POSITIVE INTIMACY

Make it work for you with this unique new guidebook!

"Nature has built into us what it takes to enjoy intimacy," says Dr. Richard Austin, "and the psychological sciences have given us the tools to use these inborn sources."

Let Dr. Austin help you to use both nature and science to increase your happiness and pleasure. With his wonderful new book you can apply the same techniques that he has used with more than a thousand single and married patients. You'll begin to put deep and rewarding intimacy into your life.

"Honest and relaxed discussions, with relevant 'cases' that happily never become 'histories' . . . consistently stresses the individual's inner resources, 'strength in aloneness,' as the underpinning of the vital intimacy each of us seeks and needs." —*Publishers Weekly*

How to Make It with Another Person

GETTING CLOSE, STAYING CLOSE

Richard B. Austin, Jr., Ph.D.

A KANGAROO BOOK

PUBLISHED BY POCKET BOOKS NEW YORK

HOW TO MAKE IT WITH ANOTHER PERSON

Macmillan edition published 1976

POCKET BOOK edition published July, 1977

This POCKET BOOK edition includes every word contained in the original, higher-priced edition. It is printed from brand-new plates made from completely reset, clear, easy-to-read type.
POCKET BOOK editions are published by
POCKET BOOKS,
a Simon & Schuster Division of
GULF & WESTERN CORPORATION
1230 Avenue of the Americas,
New York, N.Y. 10020.
Trademarks registered in the United States
and other countries.

ISBN: 0-671-81108-8.
Library of Congress Catalog Card Number: 75-35600.

Printed in the U.S.A.

Acknowledgments

Special thanks are due Nancy Bagby for her talented editing and typing of the manuscript.

Christy Coke, Claudia Williams, Tina Edling, and Ceale Wavell made helpful comments on the entire book.

My patients provided inspiration and encouragement for the conception and completion of this book.

My son, Dick, deserves special appreciation for his patience during the long hours required to write this book.

Contents

Foreword

Every human being needs close relationships with others. Yet it is precisely in our most intimate relationships that the majority of interpersonal problems occur. Of all the intimate relationships—parent-child, friend-friend, man-woman—none demands more of the participants than that between man and woman.

Intimacy deprivation between man and woman is one of the most serious problems of our time. Twenty-five years from now it may be recognized as an issue as destructive to public welfare as food deprivation. But at present, it is so common that we take it for granted, so obvious that we overlook it, so accepted that we consider it a normal way of life.

Simply stated, we do not know how to enjoy intimacy. Yet why is this so, when a majority of persons have the capacity?

It is important to grasp the enormity of the problem. Lack of intimacy seems a tragic flaw in a country where basic survival needs are largely satisfied. Two people, giving little thought to the choice, decide to marry or live together and believe that, somehow, things will "turn out all right." They discover problems of communication in the first year, yet continue to "exist" together without real satisfaction. Married or single, they suffer extreme frustration, and call it "trying to make a relationship work."

If we choose to be open to the truth about ourselves and our intimate relationships, gratification and fulfillment can be the norm in the future. But intimacy fulfillment requires

- the courage to look at our relationships realistically, and
- the ability to apply to our lives the scientific knowledge available.

If the reader will face fictions about intimacy, spelled out in succeeding chapters in this book, and share the quest to understand how persons and relationships function, the reward will be intimacy success.

Richard B. Austin, Jr., Ph.D.

*How
to Make It
with
Another
Person*

Introduction

Psychotherapy reveals a person at a level not discerned in the structured interviews of the usual research project. The psychotherapist, unlike the experimenter who observes at a distance, becomes involved in the world experienced by the person, and thus has first-hand knowledge. Owing to this involvement, psychotherapy provides outstanding research material.

During fifteen years as a practicing psychologist, I have studied the intimacy problems of over one thousand persons. I have shared their struggles to learn the truth about themselves and their intimacies. In sharing with them, I have repeatedly encountered a handful of fictions about intimate relationships—hangovers from the past when there was no science of human behavior. These fictions obscure reality and prevent our finding satisfying relationships.

This book is based primarily on my observations about those fictions. Its purpose is twofold:

- to identify specific fictions and spell out their destructiveness, and
- to point out the realities on which enjoyable intimacies are built.

People can have satisfying intimacy when they work through fictions and choose options that suit them.

Let's take a look at four areas of fiction which block intimacy.

First, the archaic idea that everyone should marry has had the negative effect of pushing persons into unwise relationships or burdening them with feelings of guilt or inadequacy if they choose to remain single. Giving up this destructive pattern requires that we ask whether or not to marry (or remarry) at all. There is the option to remain single and enjoy intimacy!

Second, the selection of a mate for a sustained, or even short-term, intimacy requires some know-how. There are guidelines, which will be discussed, for choosing relationships that offer a high probability of success. We hold on to fictions about the selection of an intimate to our own peril. We can choose to cut down on intimacy poverty by improving our selection of an intimate.

Third, the decision to terminate an intimacy rather than to conform to the fiction that termination equals failure can remove much deprivation. Whether the decision is to divorce if married or to end intimacy if single, the decision can open the door to new opportunities for satisfaction.

The fourth area regards several fictions which mislead those who share intimacy. These fictions create expectations which can only be disappointed, decreasing satisfaction in the relationship. Granted, there is some discomfort when fiction is given up for reality, but intimacy thrives on the truth. Intimacy is diminished when fiction is substituted for reality.

If fictions about intimacy are removed, what will fill the vacuum? There is enough knowledge now from the behavioral sciences to revolutionize intimate relationships—if that knowledge is put into practice. My sincere hope is that the guidelines presented here for the development of your intimate relationships will be not only read, but practiced.

Why not accept your right to pursue intimacy satisfaction? My firm belief is that—married or single—you will be rewarded by better intimacy.

The case histories described in this book are composites drawn from my practice but all of the names, occupations, and family relationships have been changed to insure that the identities of the patients remain concealed.

1 | Why Not Stay Single?

If you are over twenty-one and single, divorced, or widowed, you have probably been asked, "Why aren't you married?" Underlying this question is the assumption that marriage is a "natural" state, and that something is wrong with you if you are single. It is natural to want and have intimacy, and intimacy is possible whether single or married.

Although being over twenty-one and single no longer demands apology, social and family pressures are still strong in the direction of marriage. In fact, pressure to marry has trapped many in loveless relationships. If we continue to allow these pressures to push us prematurely into marriage, or to keep us in dead marriages, the intimacy deprivation in a high percentage of relationships will not change. The notion that one "ought to be married" is no more valid than the theory that one "ought to be single."

Doug is thirty-five, a successful lawyer, enjoys the company of a number of attractive and intelligent women, and has never been married. But behind his back one hears more than an occasional whisper: "Doug's never married . . . Hmmm." Either sexual deviancy or a "playboyish" instability may be suspected.

Sandy is twenty-eight, attractive, holds a responsible job in the public school system, and dates a variety of men. At parties, young married women are apt to gather and speculate about her. One rumor is that Sandy is going with a married man. Gossip also has it that a rich older man supplies the luxuries others feel she cannot afford.

Neither Doug nor Sandy can expect much approval if they remain single, especially if they live in a moderate-sized community of middle America. If they want intimacy without marriage, some form of disapproval is inevitable.

Where social pressure exists, parental pressure is usually more obvious. Parents who mean well may not be aware of the degree to which they program their sons and daughters toward marriage. They may justify their attempts to control behavior as "guidance" or the "voice of experience." Yet pressure is communicated—subtly at some times, more directly at others:

"Aren't you being a bit choosy, dear?"

"When are you going to see that nice young man [lovely girl] again?"

Many of us accept parental and social attitudes that only marriage is normal. Burdened by guilt or fear of rejection, we give in to pressure to act out the "appropriate" role and marry without personal conviction.

Something of the bitterness which may result if one acquiesces to familial, social, and internal pressure is expressed in this poem by Charleye T. Wright:

Ellen Was Single: A Sonnet on It*

"Your daughter is one lovely girl, I say,
and looks so chic, so perfect, with Jerome."
"Now, Mother wants the best for you, you know.
All those young men you fancy in array
are just not good enough. One day your home
will percolate to the stop and the go
of Jerome, that nice young man." "Ellen, hey,
your father loves you. I ask only some

---

* Used by permission.

small favors for my sacrifices. Oh,
that, soon, my grandchild will be with me. Pay
me back for all these years of work. Welcome
my dimming nights with Jerome's son." And so,
he moved through me, the tank that took Bastogne!
The hulk-green one that sulks in Rucker Park,
  alone.

The images in Mr. Wright's poem are well-meaning parents and friends who are more concerned with their own expectations of Ellen than they are with her expectations for herself. They communicate their feelings subtly, as in the lines describing how "perfect" she looks with Jerome, and not so subtly, as in the monologues of the mother and father. Although the parents describe their attempts to monitor her behavior as love, we are left with the feeling that Ellen takes little active part in choosing her lifestyle. Passively conforming to her parents' expectations and refusing to take a stand, she experiences her integrity as violated.

Jerome also allows himself to be trapped. Note the suggestion that he is insensitive, isolated, heavily defended, and, like Ellen, giving in to pressure to act out a role and to prove his maleness.

We may protest that this man and woman are weak and unable to resist external pressure. However, self-induced pressure is the hardest to ignore or change. From infancy, men and women absorb the expectations of persons important to them concerning their roles in life. These expectations "build in" a program of desirable behavior. The program for intimacy usually includes the mandate that marriage is the best arrangement for everyone.

Unless we become aware of the program, we have little chance of choosing not to carry out these "scripts," and less chance to write our own lines.

What do these scripts say? One of the opening lines is "Why aren't you married?"—implying that the reasons for marrying far outnumber the reasons for remaining single.

Let's examine some of the socially sanctioned reasons people marry.

First, marriage may provide a *sense of status* for both men and women. A woman acquires the title of "Mrs.," a label which in itself carries status. Her social standing increases in accordance with the prestige of her husband's position.

A man acquires status in marriage by marrying beauty, intelligence, or wealth, depending on the circles in which he moves. He may also appear more stable if he is married.

Social acceptance is another reason for marrying or staying married. The single state is particularly unacceptable to many married men and women. Single girls may find that wives are suspicious if they come within talking distance of the husbands in the room. Those divorced or widowed complain that they no longer feel welcome among their married friends.

Marriage for status or social approval is closely akin to marriage for *economic or domestic security*. Many women today still follow the historical pattern where marriage was a replacement for the early home and met their needs for food, shelter, and other basics. But marriage for economic security has a twofold negative effect. It places impossible requirements on the husband to be sole provider and substitute parent. At the same time, it strips women of their identities as persons and keeps them dependent, without the opportunity to become self-sufficient. This negative pattern works in reverse when husbands expect their wives to become surrogate mothers, meeting all their domestic needs.

However, dynamic changes are taking place in society, especially among women. These changes force us to question both the social reasons for marriage and the assumption that intimacy is normal and desirable only within marriage.

Changes in the Female Script

Changes are taking place among women in two areas. Individually, women are beginning to assume responsibility for themselves in spite of disapproval from husbands, boyfriends, employers, or women who choose the comfort of the status quo.

Growing evidence suggests that probably fewer than half of all married women can be satisfied as wives and mothers unless they engage in outside activities that furnish outlets for their talents and energies. Among women who take valid vocational interest tests, few score high in the "housewife" category.

Women are also banding together to bring about societal change through legislation. Women's organizations are gathering momentum at a rapid pace on a national scale. As women are increasingly able to maintain a good standard of living through their own work efforts, economic security becomes a less important factor in marriage.

By acting together, women are overcoming the social conditioning which for centuries has pitted them against one another as competitors for men. Such competition is a deadly trap which renders women powerless to collaborate.

Why do women need to collaborate?

All persons, whether male or female, have psychological needs for association with groups with which they share a common identity. A sense of collaboration, of working together for common goals, is important if we are to meet the psychological need for group identity.

Women also need to collaborate with men, as equals. Change in this direction may create some hostility, but hostility is a normal part of male-female relationships during a period of significant change. However, hostility will diminish when women establish separate identities, and when men accept them as equals.

Changes in the Male Script

Changes in the female script demand changes in the male script. Increasingly, more women consider marriage unnecessary. Consequently, there is pressure on males to change.

Traditionally, the relationship between men and women has been a superior-subordinate one which enhanced the male's self-esteem at the expense of the female's. This inequality is still widely accepted, despite the findings of modern psychology that there is no natural superiority of men, only natural differences between the sexes.

Because the male script dictates that superiority and authority reside with the man, he is expected to be super-adequate at all times, both on the job and at home. Such an expectation creates feelings of inadequacy; while he has been educated for his work or trained on the job so that he can cope with the demands of his position without a sense of failure, he has little training in human relations. How, then, can he skillfully make the daily shift from the highly competitive work world, where he is called upon to be aggressive, decisive, and businesslike, to the world of intimacy, where he is expected to be kind, giving, and patient?

As women become more self-sufficient, more stress is placed on the quality of intimacy and less on the status of the male. The basic pressure on men is to cease the pursuit of adequacy, and to develop the capacity for intimate relationships. There is also pressure on males to share work that used to be the woman's domain, such as cooking and caring for children.

Clearly, changes in outdated male/female models are moving both sexes out of the old scripts, toward more equality in relationships. As relationships between men and women become more equal, intimacy is more rewarding.

Interdependency

As a woman's freedom, status, and self-sufficiency increase, she becomes less dependent on a man for a sense of identity. The belief that a woman's identity is based on her relationship with a man refuses to acknowledge the separate identities of men and women. To believe that a wife is her husband's right arm or that he is her "better half" or that he is responsible for her actions, is a denial of her identity. Each is one's own person first, not an extension of someone else, and therein lies personal security. Anyone, male or female, who depends heavily upon another person for security and stability is going to be disappointed. One individual cannot create security for another, and over-dependency is a breeding ground for resentment.

But both sexes need each other. To claim no dependency is also an extreme position, and one extreme differs little from another. When there is interdependency, there is a meshing of needs. Interdependency makes real independence possible.

Strength in Aloneness

A person who has not developed sufficient inner resources to live alone undercontributes to any relationship. A person who has gained little for himself may have little to give another. As men and women develop the capacity to enjoy time apart and to use it productively, they may find that marriage as we now experience it is not necessary for internal security.

More women today require that a relationship enhance their self-respect and allow them the freedom to develop as persons. When relationships between men and women are limited by sex role expectations, the penalty is often a loss of motivation to achieve a sense of personhood and to allow the same for the other person. To develop as a person requires a person-to-person relationship rather than a role-to-role relationship. Often persons who are *not* willing to relate in a "role-free" way will find themselves left only with intimates who are afraid to be themselves.

Extrinsic reasons for marriage are being questioned in light of the demands of a person-to-person relationship. Experts tend to agree that the primary purpose of marriage today is to have intimacy needs met.

Coupled Without End?

One does not assume that an intimate relationship between *un*married persons will last forever. Yet the assumption still exists that the marriage relationship will endure until death, despite divorce records to the contrary.

Let's take a closer look at the notion of committing the rest of one's life to a relationship with a member of the opposite sex. Under careful scrutiny, some absurd aspects emerge. Can a person in his early twenties make a decision to live with another person who, according to current life-expectancy figures, may be around for another fifty to seventy years from the date of marriage?

It is difficult to make a permanent choice at any age, much less in one's early twenties. Human personalities change, relationships change, life circumstances change. At no time after adolescence do personalities change so dramatically as during the years immediately following high school or college graduation. Whole new philosophies emerge, clashing with those which have been taught by parents. The person with whom one falls in love in high school may evolve into a very different sort of being.

A marriage relationship that remains alive and caring for five decades is the exception, not the rule. The intimacy deprivation from which so many suffer in marriage would be lessened if individuals did not make the blind assumption that because they "have a good thing going" and "love each other," they must consummate the relationship in marriage.

Marriage may herald the end of the feeling that one is in a relationship because it is truly satisfying, since negative responses often emerge after the vows. As one woman recently said in a therapy group, "I don't know anymore whether I give because I choose to or because I am married." Postponing marriage, or giving it up entirely in favor of remaining single, is one way to keep intimacy alive.

* * *

Whether marriage is approached as a means or an end is vitally important. Either marriage was made for man and woman, or man and woman were made for marriage. If we value marriage above the well-being of individuals, we will try to fit as many relationships as possible into a marriage mold. But if we are primarily concerned about the well-being of individuals, we will look at the options available for enjoying intimacy. Marriage then will become a situation in which enjoying sustained intimacy is the rule.

The time to take a stand for the right to pursue and enjoy satisfying intimate relationships is *now*. Any social force or institution which attempts to persuade persons to feel guilty about ending dead relationships, or about being single, should be opposed.

Let's begin rewriting the script for sustained intimacy and reverse the pressure.

Instead of "Why aren't you married?" let's ask "Why not stay single?"

2 | How to Select a Compatible Intimate

The magic belief that "marriages are made in heaven" obscures our objectivity, and we usually choose a mate without much attention to selection factors.

Psychologists skilled in executive selection for industry state that personnel selection is over 50 percent of job success. Tests and in-depth interviews are used to select persons for key positions. Yet to assess a possible intimate in such a way seems cold, mechanical, and impersonal.

Selecting the wrong intimate in the first place exacts a heavy toll in human suffering, and needlessly so, since most mistakes can be avoided. The selection variables in this chapter are important to relationships. It is better to ask the right questions before deciding on marriage or sustained intimacy, but it is never too late. Check out a potential mate or a current intimate to see how your relationship stacks up.

DATING

"Isn't being in love, and not wanting to leave each other, enough for marriage?"

No; there are many people one can love, have an exciting relationship with, and wish never to leave.

Selection of a marital partner requires a far more careful, systematic, and deliberate approach. That is why a close look at selection factors is important.

> *"We have been going with each other for a year. Are we ready for marriage?"*

Unfortunately, the assumption that a couple who spends a great deal of time together knows each other better and therefore makes a better choice is not well grounded. Certainly, it is possible to learn more about somebody over a longer period of time, but dating rarely simulates marital conditions. The cry, "Why can't you be the way you were when we were dating?" suggests that dating practices are not those of marriage and create unrealistic expectations about marriage.

Dating, or "going together," is psychologically different from marriage. When people do not live together and share responsibilities, it is difficult to know what will happen in sustained intimacy. The business side of the relationship and the other obligations that hover over people in marriage have not yet emerged. While lengthy dating will produce a greater tolerance for intimacy problems, length alone does not indicate that the relationship is sound enough for a long-range commitment.

AGE

> *"Is age important in mate selection?"*

Age is one of the factors in marital choice. Different generations have different value systems, and marked differences in age may increase incompatibility. However, to see age in context requires that one look carefully at the other selection factors.

Psychological age is not always the same as chronological age. "Psychological age" involves a person's ability to change, degree of involvement or isolation from others, drive, ability to relate to people who are different, and span and depth of interests. A sense of purpose or direction, a capacity for intimacy, and some skill in human relations are more important than actual age difference in marriage. These factors, referred to as psychological, are basic to two persons' enjoyment of each other.

*"I am over ten years older than my boyfriend.
Should we marry?"*

Although social sanction is strongest against an older female marrying a younger male, there is no biological or psychological reason why age difference alone should be a major deterrent. Of course, the physical health and personality of the individuals involved is a factor. Individual parts of the body (skin, internal organs, and overall physical health) may be "older" or "younger" than chronological age would indicate. We know persons who are "old" at thirty or "young" at seventy.

June at thirty-eight is a lively person who enjoys her work with teenagers who have drug problems. She is active, in good physical shape, and gravitates toward people in their early twenties. In fact, her value system is humanistic and "new generation."

Bill, age twenty-four, works with the same group. He likes to sail and play the guitar with June, and to talk about their mutual cases. He is not disturbed by the fact that she is fourteen years older. Sexually, they have an outstanding relationship. Bill loves June as a person, and as he shares with her, their physical attraction increases. Neither Bill nor June wants children of their own, but would like to take disturbed teenagers into their home, or eventually adopt children of racial origins different from their own.

In spite of their compatibility, however, June feels she is too much older than Bill to marry him. Her "culture tape," which tells her that marriage to a younger man is a mistake, keeps her from seeing that their relationship meets most of the criteria for a satisfying marriage.

They have purposes that converge; yet because of strong social forces, she believes marriage is impractical.

After a year of psychotherapy, June and Bill's relationship has continued to develop. June has worked through social sanctions about age. Their relationship is a growing one with open communication and a sharing of interests.

Will they marry? Their relationship may evolve into marriage eventually, and June no longer opposes it. But they are enjoying the present intimacy fully and no longer feel a need to be concerned about the future.

COMMITMENT TO GROWTH

"If my intimate doesn't consider personal growth important, will this affect our relationship?"

Commitment to personal growth has everything to do with the length of time an intimacy remains alive and vital. Commitment to growth—willingness to learn about self and others—says something about a person's intention to live fully. Experience in psychology and in life tells us that a lack of commitment to learning results in sterile relationships and unhappy individuals.

Jane and her husband were always together. During twenty years of marriage she depended almost totally on his help and direction. At age fifty-two she had few developed personality resources.

When her husband died, she isolated herself, started drinking to ease the pain, and eventually became dependent on alcohol. She transferred her dependency from her deceased mate to the bottle.

Neither Jane nor her husband had any concept of personality development. They supported non-growth in each other and thought theirs was a "good" marriage. Jane abdicated personal responsibility for her growth, choosing instead the comfort of the status quo.

Choosing to avoid personality development in order to maintain the present state of a marriage is not placing first things first. A living, growing relationship requires that each mate take his personal development seriously.

"Is rate of personal growth important?"

Rate of growth has much to do with how well an intimacy can survive over a long period. Success in intimacy is not measured by whether or not a couple stays together, but by the degree of enjoyment and caring that exists within the relationship. If either person grows at a much faster rate than the other, conflict can be the result, unless one is willing to wait while the other makes an extra effort to "catch up." This "catching up" may be done with the help of psychotherapy or stimulating changes in the environment (a new job, shift in responsibility at home, etc.).

"Do situations help determine the rate of personal growth?"

None of us develops in a vacuum. From infancy, an individual develops his potential in dynamic interaction with people and situations around him. If one mate is exposed to stimulating situations which require him to respond and use his capabilities, he will tend to grow at a faster rate than a mate who has little opportunity to grow and learn. Much of the time, for example, highly educated, intelligent women become relatively isolated after marriage and do not pursue learning and growth commensurate with their abilities. IQ losses can result from this, according to some studies. On the other hand, these same women, when allowed opportunities for learning, tend to increase their IQs over a period of time.

Ann, an attractive mother of two children, is married to Jim, a successful and intelligent business executive. Somewhat shy, Ann rarely involved herself in social situations outside the home. Jim, on the other hand, was personable and outgoing and had made many social and business friends over the years. He was a promising young executive with potential for the highest position in his company.

Although Ann looked fine in the background, Jim was dissatisfied with her personality growth. He felt that he had been growing and changing while she had remained relatively static over the last eight or ten years. Ann admitted that she had been preoccupied with the children and house and had avoided learning situations.

As a result of their conversation, Ann became more interested in psychotherapy to stimulate her development. During therapy, she began to realize that part of her passivity was due to the way she perceived her mother: docile and unwilling to grow. She recognized that her lack of self-confidence was the result of unconscious lessons from her mother on how to be a woman.

She decided that she didn't want to continue in the old ways—that she wanted to take risks, to understand herself better, and to develop her potential. And she began to develop at a noticeably faster pace. Impatient for progress, she entered group therapy as well. Risking openness with the group and allowing them to give her positive feedback helped her build self-esteem and the sense of affirmation she had not been able to achieve with her parents.

With continued therapy, Ann gained self-confidence. She completed a course in modeling and, on her own initiative, got a job with a local television station doing commercials. Her sense of confidence from her achievements has brought considerable inner satisfaction. Her growth rate is at least equal to her husband's now—to his satisfaction as well as her own.

ATTITUDES TOWARD OTHERS

"My fiancé doesn't trust people; I do. Is this important to our relationship?"

Yes, very important. Trust is essential for an intimate relationship. A person who distrusts widely will probably be intolerant. Since intimacy involves self-exposure, mates have ample opportunity to find reasons to distrust, which builds a barrier to intimacy.

INTRINSIC VALUES

"I like to enjoy our friends, while my husband likes to socialize to help his business. What can we do to resolve the difference?"

On the surface, this question suggests a basic difference in attitudes toward people. However, social relationships meet many needs, and a sense of purpose in a relationship can make it more meaningful. If promoting business activities is that purpose, manipulation need not be the goal; your husband may also enjoy the company. Several needs may be met by a single relationship. If, however, one mate is primarily oriented toward using people and the other is oriented toward relating in a warm, helpful way, serious problems can emerge. A difference in values becomes the issue.

Something is valued intrinsically when it is valued for its own sake instead of for external reasons. Appreciation for art, for example, is an intrinsic value if one collects paintings for their beauty instead of their resale value. Intrinsic values are important to consider before entering a committed relationship, since what you value will determine how you budget money, spend leisure time, choose friends, or select a vocation.

"Do intrinsic values change much over time?"

Usually, one develops a personal value system, whether consciously or unconsciously, during adolescence. Surprisingly little change occurs after the age of twenty-one. At one time in life a person may become interested in political activities because of interest in some cause, or a person may have a religious experience which will cause a reorientation of values. But basic values remain essentially the same.

However, a value system may not be put into action until after marriage—and with severe consequences to the relationship. Tom's wife Marilyn was ambitious and economically oriented. When Tom, at twenty-three, decided to enter the ministry because he wanted to "help people and serve God," Marilyn's world crumbled. She could not accept, or live with, the lifestyle that resulted from Tom's value system. Although Tom was not engaged in religious activity before marriage, he scored high in that area on a test which measures values.

Obviously, it is important to clarify differences in intrinsic values before marriage, and to discuss how differences might affect behavior in a variety of life situations.

SENSITIVITY TO FEELINGS

"My feelings are frequently hurt. Am I too sensitive?"

If you are a person whose feelings are often hurt, you need to understand that you are highly sensitive, and to realize that people are not trying to hurt you. One who is highly sensitive often expects others to be equally sensitive, and suspects them of trying to hurt feelings deliberately when they are not. Accept extra sensitivity and use it to be aware of other persons.

"Do I need a mate who is equally sensitive?"

Rapport between intimates is greater if they are nearly equal in sensitivity to feelings in themselves and others. Mates can be equally sensitive, however, and show that sensitivity in different ways. One mate, for example, may overreact slightly to small nuances in conversation with an intimate, while the other, although equally sensitive, may put a brake on his own reaction.

Awareness of your own special areas of sensitivity is a step toward minimizing overreaction to others. An open, accepting discussion of touchy areas is the best remedy for healing emotional wounds and preventing them from being reopened in the future. If communication is immediate when feelings are hurt, intimates have a chance to prevent the situation's recurrence.

I am reminded of a patient who was highly sensitive and was always slightly depressed. She seemed to carry the weight of the past and present on her shoulders. She had experienced much injury in a relationship with parents who were apparently not as sensitive as she, and each new relationship was a fresh opportunity for salt to be rubbed into old wounds.

Already bruised and feeling inadequate from past experience, she cringed from even subtle criticism. After psychotherapy, however, she became much less sensitive to what others said and did, and, even when hurt, was more aware of their real intentions. Even so, this patient —in order to risk being open—still needed intimacies with persons who were as sensitive as herself.

EDUCATION

"Is education related to marital success?"

Yes and no. Statistics show that there is a lower divorce rate among college graduates than among high school graduates. Yet factors other than education— such as the facts that college graduates marry later, earn more money, and are more likely to seek professional help with problems—could explain those statistics.

Granted, exposure to a college campus for four years usually involves some learning about human relationships and a chance to view different philosophical approaches to life. But too often there is little learning about how to live successfully with other people. It is time colleges assumed more responsibility for providing learning experiences to help people live constructively in small groups, and in the larger social milieu.

"How about differences in education between intimates?"

Studies indicate that most wives want their husbands to have at least as much education as they have, if not more. But if the husband has advanced degrees while the wife has a high school education, the differences could cause some problems if the wife feels insecure about her education. The majority of husbands wish wives to have equal education, and a minority want them to have less. It seems to be a hard pill for a male to swallow if his wife has more education than he does. Generally, if education tends to be equal, both parties tend to be happier.

If a mate who lacks formal education is willing to learn, however, there may be no problem. Ken, for example, has a doctorate in American history. Diane never finished college because she went to work to put him through school. But Diane has made it a point to keep up with Ken by keeping alive her interest in politics. Because she is motivated to learn, she is able to help him with his research and class lectures by scanning articles he doesn't have time to read. She is also an active member of the local League of Women Voters and the state women's political caucus. Thus, she continues to grow in the relationship.

SOCIAL COMPATIBILITY

"Is it a potential problem that my fiancée does not like most of my friends?"

It certainly can be. Friends are chosen on the basis of many conscious and unconscious factors in personality.

Margaret, age twenty-two, has been going with Bill, age twenty-seven, for two years. After two years in the army he is completing a master's degree in business management. She is graduating in June with a bachelor of arts degree in literature and social studies. Margaret's friends prefer to discuss current events in depth, the latest books, or social issues. Bill is bored by this conversation. He reads the sports page of the newspaper and the stock reports. He chooses friends who like to watch football and play golf.

This relationship might work if Margaret and Bill do not force their friends on each other. But if their close friends do not get along, it could indicate that Bill and Margaret do not have much in common. This fact may be obscured by the camouflage of romantic love. Three years from now one can visualize Bill glued to the TV, watching football all weekend, while Margaret tries to read a book with a small child pulling at her dress. There are "his" friends and "her" friends, and no friends in common.

Although it may be healthy to have friends not shared by your mate, going too far in this direction could lead to a two-world existence. Bill could learn more about literature and Margaret grasp the fundamentals of football, so that the two of them could move toward a common social network.

"Should I listen to the opinion of friends about my girlfriend (boyfriend)?"

Yes. The judgment of several good friends who have your welfare in mind is an objective check on the "blind spots" in your relationship. Friends are likely to be more objective about your intimate than you are.

The decision is yours, of course, but friends can offer you important information for consideration. On the other hand, unsolicited opinions are a waste of time if you are not receptive.

SOCIO-ECONOMIC BACKGROUND

"In an age of tolerance, do socio-economic factors matter when a couple is in love?"

It would be progress if socio-economic factors did not matter. Categorizing people by social class explains little because it doesn't tell us much about the person.

But when a couple marries, they must agree on a way of life; and lifestyle is affected by socio-economic status. In short, different classes have different habits.

Of course, if there are genuine growth possibilities in a relationship, even major differences in this area might not be formidable. Still, major differences are usually a handicap instead of an asset and should be examined objectively.

AUTHORITY

"He makes the important decisions and I make the others. Isn't this one way to divide authority?"

This is one way to divide authority, but not to share it. Ideally, sharing authority on the basis of time and talent is preferable in marriage. When one person has aptitude in a particular area, such as bookkeeping, he should be allowed to function in that area without interference. On the other hand, he needs to be aware that a mild form of autocracy can exist if he does not communicate what he is doing. It might be important for intimates to discuss, both before and after marriage, such matters as keeping a check book and budgeting, regardless of who will have the primary responsibility for monitoring finances.

"Is a fifty-fifty authority arrangement possible?"

Such an arrangement may be ideal, but it is rarely possible. There is a tendency for one person to be more dominant than the other in a relationship, according to expertise and energy. Deciding where authority should reside on the basis of sex is an outdated solution.

"What authority do I give up as a person when I get married?"

The answer to that is clear: Only the authority you want to give up. Any person in an intimate relationship who abdicates rights in order to preserve intimacy is giving up authority that is rightfully his own. Whenever one person's interests are at stake and the other person opposes those rights, one can mobilize authority and take a definite stand. For example, when two persons planning marriage decide that they both want to complete their education, they can decide through discussion that one will work while the other goes to school, then vice-versa, or both may be able to attend school and work. Both are thus exercising individual authority toward the achievement of goals.

COMMUNICATION

"I'm afraid she doesn't tell me what she really thinks or feels. Is there anything I can do to bring her out?"

Trying to guess what a mate wants is like swimming in murky waters. If your mate expects you to know what she needs without her telling you, she is laboring under the illusion that because you love her you will be able to read her mind. You may become frustrated trying to second-guess, and non-communication will lead to misunderstanding.

To help her express her feelings, do not reward her for saying what you want to hear unless she actually believes it. If you suspect that she is leveling with you, thank her for being open and honest, even if you don't like what she thinks.

If she is not sure how she feels, talk about your feelings and ideas, and she may become more in touch with herself. Try not to assume that you know how your intimate thinks or feels. If one concentrates on paying attention to feelings and thoughts, expression will improve. Ask your mate questions about where she is until she tells you of her own accord.

"Suppose we have not really communicated with each other for some time. How can we start?"

If there has been an absence of communication for some time, problems usually pile up. The best place to start is in the areas where the strongest feelings exist. Assess the sensitive spots in a relationship, those areas that are most difficult to talk about—a mother-in-law you don't like, your dislike for being dominated, or your resentment of your mate's procrastination. Begin by structuring the situation. Agree that the two of you need to talk about matters that are important, though emotionally charged, and set up a time to talk that is agreeable to both of you. Then talk.

Let's look at what can happen when couples do not communicate for a long period of time. An impasse is established. Betty, after six years of marriage, says, "He just reads the newspaper when I try to discover why he is cold with me." John, on the other hand, says, "Betty is never happy anymore. It's no fun doing things together. All we share now are duties and responsibilities." At this point, John does not want to discuss problems. Betty feels rejected and shut out of the relationship.

Betty and John have let problems slide by for years, and a wall has been erected between them. Communication now will be painful, which is one reason John avoids telling Betty how he feels. Yet, if the pain is not experienced and feelings are not communicated directly, there will only be a legal marriage and no actual closeness.

If Betty and John had seen a therapist before marriage, they might have explored how the inevitable problems of intimacy could be faced and worked through by talking openly. Sensitive areas for each of them could have been faced.

John and Betty need to learn to express feelings to each other in a non-critical way. But he is not totally responsible for her happiness and should not feel guilty when he senses her dissatisfaction. Betty blames her dissatisfaction on the marriage, which, in her case, is an indication that she set marriage, and not personal growth, as the primary goal in life. She is bound to use marriage as the scapegoat when anything goes wrong.

Actually, Betty needs to listen to herself in order to understand what she really wants and needs. She doesn't know herself well enough to realize that marriage alone cannot make her happy. She needs other activities, or a job, where she can use her talents.

Unless Betty can be helped to understand herself and John can learn to listen to Betty instead of avoiding her, their marriage will become increasingly sterile.

If partners cannot discuss sensitive areas, routine problems cannot be solved.

AUTHENTICITY

"Sometimes she doesn't seem real to me. She is always so pleasant and polite."

Surface charm, saying the right thing, and smiling on cue comprise some people's social personality. Sally, for example, makes friends easily by clever conversation, but there is little of the "real" Sally for anyone to see. If she drops the facade in a close relationship, role playing with others may not block intimacy. If she does not, beware: Sally may be unaware of who she really is.

"Sometimes I wonder if I know him, since his words and actions often conflict."

Consistency of verbal expression and behavior is one measure of authenticity. One man tells his wife he loves her but rarely shows it by deeds. A woman tells all of her "secrets" in great detail but omits the most important revelation: herself.

Authenticity is related to self-awareness much as a compass is to a steering wheel: being authentic establishes direction while self-awareness helps keep one on a course that expresses the real personality.

SELF-AWARENESS

"I am not sure how I really feel about any-thing or anyone."

Sit down and think through your feelings, either alone or with a trusted friend. In so doing, you may be surprised to discover that you have no "pure" feelings, that your feelings are mixed—toward yourself, your spouse, or your intimate. This idea will be confusing until you understand that it is impossible to avoid mixed feelings toward yourself and those close to you.

You are the exception if you have not experienced every emotion on the spectrum toward yourself at one time or another. At times, we are angry with ourselves, anxious about our behavior, happy or unhappy with ourselves, or feel threatened by our own wishes or actions.

How we feel about ourselves with an intimate will tell us a lot about what is going on in the relationship. If we find ourselves trying too hard to please a mate, we may discover either that we are receiving little actual acceptance from the other person, or that we have difficulty in receiving acceptance.

"How can I handle my angry feelings in a relationship?"

Understanding anger is a vital part of intimacy, and angry feelings exist in any active relationship.

It is not uncommon for persons to repress or block feelings of irritation, since they are considered socially unacceptable. A frequent sign of underlying anger is retreat. Since an intimate is usually the first person to feel the brunt of your repressed feelings, you can expect anger in return.

To get in touch with your feelings, accept the fact that anger is inevitable. Then, make a list of the things that might irritate you. Simply writing them down may help you discover the source of your anger. Being aware of what makes you angry will help you control your expression of anger. If you remain unaware of or do not accept your angry feelings, those feelings may be expressed in camouflaged ways which are beyond your control.

SELF-ESTEEM

"I don't think I like myself very well."

The extent to which we think well of ourselves is what is meant by self-esteem, and low self-esteem can spell problems in a relationship. If there is a high degree of self-dislike, that dislike may cause us to find more and more that we dislike about our intimate. The corollary is also true: The more we like ourselves, the more we are able to like our intimate.

It is a tragedy that people have such resistance to saying good things about themselves. Even in psychotherapy groups, where there is no taboo against self-expression, people are reluctant to discuss their good qualities.

Try it yourself. Say two or three good things about yourself to others, and watch their reaction. Almost immediately they will think you are conceited, or that you consider yourself superior to them. We are conditioned not to speak well of, or even feel good about, ourselves. Even when the praise comes from others, we tend to be suspicious, saying to ourselves, "I wonder what he wants."

Despite this conditioning, however, and regardless of what has happened to you in the past, self-esteem can be built. Liking oneself is an essential ingredient for mental health and a measure of one's capacity to like others.

If you are interested in increasing your self-esteem,

try this exercise. Ask yourself, "What is my image of myself?" Picture yourself physically—from your face to your feet. Do you like what you see? If you don't, can you do something about it, such as lose weight, or change hairstyles? If so, why not try it? Changing yourself on the outside may be the first step in changing yourself inside.

Now picture yourself in a room full of people. How do they react to you as a person? Do they tend to feel positive toward you? Do you expect them to be positive with you? If there are negative feelings, what seems to be behind the negative feelings? Do you find that people tend to ignore you or react in a lukewarm way? Is this what you want, or would you like their reactions to change? The way people react to you has a lot to do with your self-esteem.

How do you see yourself in that room full of people? What are the qualities you like best about yourself in social situations? What are the qualities you like least? In other words, what builds your self-esteem, and what lowers your self-esteem? If you find that you have certain characteristics which do nothing for your self-esteem, you have the option of dropping them. For example, if being friendly with others builds your self-esteem, being friendly will be important to you. Even when you don't feel like it, you will do what is necessary to build your self-esteem.

Be honest with yourself about the things that lower your self-esteem. Look for the payoff and decide whether it is worth the loss of self-appreciation.

"Is it possible to not know what I think of myself?"

If you mean that there is such a thing as an unconscious level of self-esteem, the answer is yes. A person usually acts in response to a composite of two self-images: a conscious one (an image he is immediately aware of), and an unconscious one (an image he is not immediately aware of). The unconscious self-image has a powerful effect on behavior.

Bud is twenty-six years old and has a history of drug problems, brushes with the law, and job failures. During hypnotherapy he expressed his unconscious self-image through a drawing that resembled Satan, and wrote the word "devil" across the drawing. A brief history revealed that his family was hostile toward him and told him, "You never do anything right. You are a disgrace to the family." He became convinced of this and acted it out, unaware of this unconscious image of himself.

Once he was convinced that he had been used as a pawn for family aggression, and that he could now choose to live his life and not his family's, he was able to begin a new life. So far he has not returned to his old self-image, or to the self-defeating behavior which was a result of this self-image.

Discovering how you feel about yourself at an unconscious level is difficult. One technique is to draw your self-image in a freeform style. Give your imagination free rein in interpreting your image. By so doing, you will get in touch with unconscious ideas you have about yourself.

In one group therapy session we talked about our unconscious self-image under hypnosis. When all the members had reached a fairly deep level of hypnosis, they visualized themselves in various ways and in turn discussed the unconscious aspects of their self-image. One woman who was bright and outgoing saw herself as isolated and alone in a darkened room. However, she saw light at a distance and was moving toward the light. The light, we learned later, represented her efforts to be more aware of herself.

In spite of the fact that there was no obvious reason for low self-esteem, the center of this woman's personality revealed that a low level of self-esteem had caused her to isolate herself as a means of protection at an early age. When two other members of the group offered to join her in the darkened area her anxieties were reduced. She no longer felt alone.

TOLERANCE OF INTIMACY

*"Doesn't the fact that we are in love indicate
that we can tolerate sustained intimacy?"*

Definitely not. Certainly, love is the epitome of an involved feeling for another, but living with someone on a daily basis demands more than love. Individuals differ tremendously in tolerance of intimacy. For example, if your mate says, "I really want to be with you," but rarely allows adequate time for intimacy, he or she may be unconsciously saying that he cannot tolerate as much intimacy as he thinks. Of course, tolerance for intimacy is not static; but the extent to which one can share time, feelings, and ideas is a measure of tolerance of intimacy.

On the other hand, the amount of time spent together may not be an accurate measure of how much intimacy one can tolerate, since some persons function in a distant manner, with little interpersonal contact. Actually, one's ability to allow separateness with an intimate is a measure of how well one can tolerate intense intimacy. The experience of separateness often allows more intense intimacy without a feeling of suffocation.

To discover your tolerance for intimacy with a given person, picture yourself in a scene with someone you know. Imagine the two of you moving toward each other without speaking. Be aware at what point you become uncomfortable. Practice this same exercise with real people. Remember that physical closeness is one way of expressing tolerance for emotional closeness. Keep in mind, however, that you are expressing the degree of emotional closeness you can tolerate with a given individual, since some people are able to tolerate physical closeness with very little emotional investment. This exercise sets the scene for an interesting discussion of the feelings behind one's actions.

"How can I rate myself and my intimate on compatibility?"

With pencil and mate in hand, you may want to go over the following checklist to see how many of the criteria for a good marriage or intimacy you and your mate have. Rate your relationship as honestly as possible, and have your mate do the same. Then compare notes. The comparison itself will tell you a great deal about your differences.

These guidelines are not a psychological test, since a test would require standardization procedures. However, based on the samples of couples I have observed, those who have fulfilling marriages and who are experiencing marital improvement have more scores at points 4 and 5.

If you are not yet married and your self-rating falls below the median (or 3) score on a majority of the guidelines, you and your intimate may have serious problems of incompatibility. If this is the case, make every effort to discover what they are, or consult a psychotherapist for help. If you are already married and see that major incompatibility exists, discuss the areas that are causing problems. Differences between intimates can enliven a relationship with understanding.

COMPATIBILITY CHART

Intimate Selection Factors	Very Different	Somewhat Different	Undecided Whether Different or Similar	Somewhat Similar	Very Similar
	1	2	3	4	5
Age					
Commitment to Growth					
Attitudes Toward People					
Social Compatibility					
Sensitivity to Feelings					
Education					
Intrinsic Values					
Socio-Economic Background					
Authority					
Communication					
Authenticity					
Self-Awareness					
Tolerance of Intimacy					

3 | You Can Only Be Yourself Well

The core of the "let me remake you" fiction is that one has the right to decide how an intimate should behave as a human being. In addition to destroying pleasure in a relationship, this illusion erodes the ground on which growth in intimacy takes place.

Yet this fiction is so common that "let me remake you" attitudes follow intimates through the years, destroying self-esteem. Since personality, as well as intimacy, thrives on the experience of being accepted, "remaking" works against positive change in people.

Why do so few escape the snares of this fiction?

Each of us seems to have a drive to perfect himself. Related to this drive is a wish to perfect our environment, including the people around us. The drive itself is not destructive, but the expression of it as "let me remake you" creates a climate where vital communication breaks down. Once this fiction is perceived as an anathema to intimacy, we can work together toward an intimacy that will bring out the best in us and our intimates.

Psychotherapy patients have provided information about this fiction that tells us more about its origins. Countless patients gradually become aware, after they learn to listen to themselves, that unrealistic expectations for an intimate have roots in childhood.

Granted, parents make their share of mistakes. But some of the anger children feel toward parents is the result of disappointed expectations. These expectations are often carried over into intimacy so that the intimate becomes the target of anger or disappointment when he or she does not conform to a standard of perfection.

Let's look at some of the ways people caught up in this fiction express themselves.

- "I am angry at you for not being the romantic lover I need."
- "You have disappointed me in so many ways."
- "You are so often not as considerate as I would like you to be."
- "Sometimes I want to hit you. You stubbornly refuse to change, even though the change is for your own good."
- "I have tried everything to please you, and nothing works."

As intimates learn to express disappointments, the way is paved to modify attempts to remake each other. Discharging anger because a mate is not ideal brings relief and allows for the development of a human-to-human relationship.

Let's look at how one person faced her desire to remake her mate, and how she changed, thus helping to create an intimacy that was therapeutic for both of them.

After a year of marriage, a young wife was experiencing growing disappointment about her husband's reactions to a variety of social situations. He didn't want to get involved, as she did, in social groups, club work, or with neighbors and friends. He had been introverted before they married, but she had assumed that she could bring him out.

She remembered a consultation with their minister prior to marriage. He had told her, "It's amazing how people change after the first year of marriage." She had mistakenly inferred from the pastor's remarks that her husband would change, after marriage, into the type of person she had dreamed he would be—outgoing and sociable.

She did perceive personality patterns in her husband before marriage that were not acceptable to her. But she was unrealistic in assuming that her husband would become more gregarious after marriage. During psychotherapy she began to understand that her underlying feelings of resentment and disappointment were communicated to him in a negative way, and were also contributing to his further withdrawal from social involvement. He sensed that he was not acceptable in her eyes.

As she began to accept him as he was, her anxieties about his not "performing correctly" in public were lessened. She reduced pressure for change, and he began to feel less threatened, because he did not have to conform to a social mold he did not fit. As a result, he was able to relax, and gradually become less reserved with friends.

This wife had begun to understand a basic principle of personality: "You can only be yourself well." The corollary of this principle is: "No other person can be you as well as you can." When these principles are understood by intimates, it is easier for them to see each other as unique human beings. There is no longer any need to compare an intimate either with one's ideal expectations or with other persons. Would you expect a lily to grow from a rose seed?

What happens when one is unable to see the real person?

Perceptual Distortion of Intimates

By the time intimates seek professional help, they often have lost so much objectivity that each sees the other in caricature.

Distortion of reality often occurs in intimacy, since objectivity is more difficult where strong emotions are involved. Negative feelings may inundate an intimate and wash away trust and good will, leaving an image that distorts the real person. If one or the other intimate does not regain realistic perception, distortions may become entrenched, sometimes requiring the intervention of a psychotherapist.

I have asked people to describe both the positive and negative aspects of an intimate, in order to clarify their perception as a basis for discussion of distortion. It is also helpful for an intimate to describe himself or herself by the use of adjectives.

Although in actual practice questionnaires may be used, people can generally assess themselves accurately, using their own words to describe both positive and negative aspects of their personality. Try it for yourself and see. How would you describe your mate and yourself? Where do you and your intimate disagree on self-ratings, or on mate ratings? Discuss with your mate the way you describe yourself and look at areas of disagreement between the two of you. Discussion can help clarify areas of distortion.

Next, ask yourself how you would like to be in an ideal sense. Follow this with a request that your intimate specify and list how she/he would like for you to change. If you are feeling mate pressure to change, you will be able to identify the direction of the pressure. Then you can bring disappointments out in the open with less chance of harming the relationship and with a greater opportunity to resolve differences.

Let's look at a psychotherapy case where serious perceptual disagreements are taking place.

The husband describes himself as warm, giving, outgoing, assertive, and a leader, while his wife describes him as critical, a perfectionist, dominant, and controlling.

The same wife sees herself as basically shy, sensitive, aware, and passive, while her husband perceives her as isolated, negative, and passive-dominant.

Each intimate sees the other as somewhat critical and dominant. When their relationship began to deteriorate, much criticism actually did take place, so that each was experiencing the other as negative. In a situation like this, negative aspects of an intimate may be magnified and positive traits overlooked until each sees the other in caricature. In the midst of conflict, objectivity is difficult.

This couple can begin to correct distortions, firstly, by looking at themselves from the other's point of view. The husband can recognize that what he considers withdrawal, his intimate sees as shyness. The wife, feeling understood, may recognize that at times she does withdraw. Her husband can see that at times he seems dominant when he means to be assertive. Also, he might admit that he tends to be more critical at home than he is with others.

Secondly, each person can start to understand that the way they experience each other is not realistic. The husband, who at times seems critical and domineering, has other personality traits. There are times when he expresses warmth and friendliness.

Thirdly, the couple can discuss interaction. As her husband becomes more critical, the wife becomes increasingly negative and thus fulfills her husband's perception of her. As she becomes more negative-dominant, he in turn grows increasingly less friendly. Each is responsible for his or her contribution to their problems.

Fourthly, a careful evaluation of behavior and what it means can further modify perceptual distortions. For example, what seems negative-dominant behavior to his wife may in fact be a managerial approach to problems of disorganization. The meaning of specific actions must be openly discussed, since misunderstandings feed perceptual distortion.

It may also be necessary to discharge negative feelings before the other's point of view can be explored. Because of the negative perception each mate has, negative feelings are inevitable. In the case of the couple just described, joint interviews where each mate listened to the feelings and perceptions of the other were enough to start the process of listening more objectively to the other person.

As the intimates saw each other more objectively and realized how they wanted each other to change, the direction of attempts to remake the other became clear. Descriptions 1 and 2 depict how the husband ideally wants to be, and how his wife wants him to be ideally.

1		2	
Husband's		Wife's	
Ideal Self-Description		Ideal Husband Description	
	Considerate		Considerate
	Independent		Generous
	Managerial		Warm
	Generous		Friendly
Bossy		Passive	
	Warm		
Negative	Positive	Negative	Positive

The husband's ideal self is primarily warm, yet independent and managerial. His ideal self differs from his wife's ideal of him in the area of strong leadership. She wants him to be more passive, less dominant. Note that he wants to be positive-assertive, while his wife wants him to be more positive-passive.

Comparison of the wife's ideal self and her husband's ideal for her follows. Her ideal self is close to the husband's ideal for her, except that he wants her to be more passively positive and giving, while she wants to be more positive-assertive.

3		4	
Wife's		Husband's	
Ideal Self-Description		Ideal Wife Description	
	Generous		Generous
	Very Warm		Very Warm
	Giving		
	Friendly	Passive	
	Cooperative	Compliant	
Negative	Positive	Negative	Positive

Actually, the discrepancy between ideals is minor, but the issue could be major. Does he not want her to be more assertive as a person? They will need to discuss this, or he may block her growth or try to "remake her" in a more positive-passive image.

These descriptions are a means of clarifying the way intimates see themselves and each other, and how each would like to change and see change. Spelling out realities allows intimates to discuss real differences and avoid fictitious views of each other.

Idol Worship

The opposite of wanting to remake an intimate is to believe that the intimate is already ideal. Instead of "Let me remake you to fit my ideal," the intimate is now saying "You are perfect as you are." This view subverts acceptance of the real person as effectively as do efforts to remake, since acceptance is given for an image, not an individual. Such a view is close to idol worship.

Norma, for example, always finds an excuse for her husband's actions because she believes that he is always right. By establishing a relationship with a man she thinks of as "perfect," she hopes to compensate for her own feelings of inferiority.

However, self-esteem cannot be borrowed, nor is it contagious. In fact, Norma is beginning to resent her husband, since self-confidence suffers in marriage to a "god." Her dependency on him to supply her with self-confidence creates an unequal relationship which further adds to her feelings of unworthiness.

At times, he feels like a fraud and wants to withdraw from the relationship. He does not experience acceptance as a human being. When we treat persons as idols, we deny them the right to humanness, to imperfection. This results in an enormous burden to live up to that standard. When the "idol" is discovered to have feet of clay, Norma may be disappointed and confused. If she and her mate can face the disillusionment openly, there is a chance for them to have a better relationship.

In the case of "idol worship," the idol usually contributes to the fiction. Norma's spouse received acceptance as a child from his mother by "doing everything right." His mother overreacted to his desirable traits and did not choose to respond to his humanness. Her acceptance of him had an unreal quality. He then selected a wife who wanted a "perfect husband." Being accustomed to his mother's acceptance, based on exaggerated perception, he was comfortable with Norma. He believed that to be really accepted, he had to be an "idol" of sorts.

Idol worship is not very different from "Let me remake you." Acceptance of the intimate as an authentic person is not present in either case. Acceptance that reaches another human being cannot be dependent on whether that person can be "remade" or "worshiped."

Transference

Sometimes when patients describe a parent or sibling, and then describe their mate, it becomes obvious that a transference is taking place in the relationship. Transference occurs when a person sees characteristics in another (a mate) that he sees in a significant individual from his past (a parent) without adequate evidence to support the perception. For example, if a wife describes her mother as domineering, bossy, and critical, and then describes her husband in the same manner, a transference may be in operation. Because the wife needs to protect herself against her mother's criticism in the past, she may focus attention on similar characteristics in her husband and inflate them out of proportion.

Some transferences can be quickly corrected by

awareness and discussion. Others have such deep roots that intensive and long-term psychotherapy is needed. A year to two years is actually a short time to resolve transference problems in intimacy.

One patient refused to believe that most of her criticism of her husband was based on her relationship with her father, who had refused to give her the affection she needed. She also transferred to her therapist a tendency to withhold affection, despite her intellectual understanding of the fact that a therapist is limited in the amount of affection he/she can give.

In group psychotherapy, with five men and four women, she could not overlook her reaction to several male members of the group. As she reenacted her relationship with her father with male group members, she correctly perceived her tendency to block positive responses from them, and then to feel hurt and rejected as she had felt with her father. She used many verbal and non-verbal cues to show her resistance to male acceptance. She would turn her body away from the men in the group who showed acceptance of her. She would also ignore positive remarks by refusing to respond, by changing the subject, or by using a voice tone that implied, "You're nice, but you're not sincere." She also perceived that she reacted to female members of the group much more openly than to male members.

The multiple relationships in group psychotherapy helped this woman to correct perceptual distortion. She discovered that, as a defense, she was refusing to "receive" from men, and she also realized that not all men were incapable of giving like her father. As she learned to be receptive to genuine affirmation from male group members, she had a new experience with men from which to draw. Instead of transferring emotional reactions out of her past to her husband, she was then able to generalize from what she had learned about herself and men in group therapy and apply that knowledge to the marital relationship. In this way transference was resolved.

Acceptance Instead of Distortion

Paradoxically, the less we pressure people to change, the more aware they become of areas they need to change. Genuine acceptance modifies and/or prevents many problems in intimacy. As we relate to the "positives" in our mates, we are on the path to accepting them as they are. To our surprise, we may find that acceptance is all that is needed to stimulate them to change.

What specific steps may we take to correct perceptual distortions of an intimate?

- Admit the possibility that you may have seen your mate incorrectly.
- Face underlying feelings, such as the fear of being vulnerable in an intimate relationship.
- Be in touch with your current feelings toward your mate, and compare those with feelings you experienced at the beginning of the relationship. The greater the change, the more distortion there may be.
- Check with a mutual friend if you're not sure how your mate behaves with other persons. If several persons agree, the likelihood of perceptual error is smaller.
- If perceptual distortion exists, train your attention *away* from the distortion areas and *toward* positive aspects of the mate's personality.

By working to change *your* perception of your mate, you will be more persuasive as an advocate of positive change. An intimate who admits a desire to change, and works to change, is more convincing than someone who simply talks about change, or insists on changing another.

Facilitating Positive Growth in Intimacy

Intimacy can be a place where the damage done to self-esteem in childhood and adolescence is repaired and one's sense of self-worth is supported. This can come about if we are interested, not in remaking our mate, but in establishing a relationship where positive change unfolds naturally. In other words, intimacy is not a place for reconstruction, but an opportunity for rehabilitation and growth.

We do not have to be psychotherapists to relate to persons in ways that help them to be themselves. And being what one *can* be is my definition of positive growth.

We can all improve on:

- Supporting self-esteem.
- Communicating feelings.
- Encouraging positive change.
- Developing self-awareness.
- Supporting growth movements.
- Confronting our mates positively.

As we practice these principles in intimacy, the results will speak for themselves. Let's take a closer look at some of these principles through the concrete interactions of Judy and Keith.

Support self-esteem

Judy's husband, Keith, is a successful doctor. They fell in love when he was an intern at medical school and she was a freshman in college. Before leaving for a residency in internal medicine, he persuaded her to marry and go with him. Judy became pregnant during the first six months of marriage, and decided she could not return to school and do justice to child-rearing. Two other children followed, and Judy never returned to work or to school.

Because of the social circles in which they now move, Keith has become increasingly aware of Judy's inability to talk effectively on a broad range of topics. Knowing her potential to learn, he feels guilty about having persuaded her to leave school.

Judy herself is defensive. Saddled with the demands of three children and a large home, she resents the lack of time available for self-development. She also resents the hours Keith spends with his patients. She fears he may be withdrawing because he is bored with her.

When he comes in late from the hospital, she greets him at the door with, "You're never on time. Why didn't you call? Why do you always put your patients ahead of your family?" Angered by what seems to him an unreasonable attitude, Keith responds, "How bitchy can you be? You knew the demands on my time when you married me!"

Labeling with a bad name ("bitchy") or criticizing with a broad generalization, ("You're never on time") reduces self-esteem. Judy is already suffering damage to her self-esteem and is feeling a need to clarify her identity. Where but in a supportive intimate relationship should one be able to be open and honest, drop ego defenses, have respect, and be confident that self-esteem is safe?

Pointing out areas of irritation, without attacking the other person, requires skill, but it can be done. Judy might have said, "I get upset when you're late without calling." "I get upset" indicates that Judy has accepted responsibility for the feeling, whereas, "You're never on time" or "You make me furious" puts the blame on the partner. In saying "I get upset," she has expressed her feelings without attacking Keith as a person. Instead of counterattacking, he could have responded with, "I'm sorry I overlooked calling you," or "I'm sorry you were upset and waited for my call. It is difficult to be a doctor's wife with the demands on my time." Keith can then *act* on his caring by phoning the next time he thinks he is going to be late.

Communicate feelings

The central issue behind Judy's anger is not the cold dinner, but her growing insecurity in the face of a loss of self-esteem. Communication of feelings is essential for intimacy, yet Judy avoids direct expression of anger. Intimacy cannot survive ordinary problems without clear communication of feelings.

Wounded by their earlier outburst and feeling guilty, Keith wants to resolve the conflict indirectly by making love. "Let's make up," he says, leading her toward the bedroom.

Judy, who in the past has given in to Keith's wishes for fear of seeming cold or hurting his pride, gives in again, silently this time. Still angry, she naturally is uncommunicative and sexually unresponsive. Angered, baffled, and hurt by her behavior, Keith withdraws in silence, and an impasse occurs.

If neither partner is able to affirm the sexuality of the other at this point, destructive forces will gain momentum and there will be a lack of mutual support for individual identity. The razor's edge of the destructive force cuts into the most critical area of mental health or emotional well-being: self-esteem.

Sex is an area that can rarely be ignored for long. Yet problems with sexual communication are frequently only the tip of the iceberg. What usually needs to be changed is the basic way a couple relates. Communication is Keith and Judy's real problem.

If the silence is not broken and real feelings, however negative, are not expressed, the relationship will become inhibited by more and broader areas of non-communication until conversation becomes superficial and open disagreements rarely occur. To expect consistent agreement is unrealistic when two unique individuals live together.

If problems are faced and communication—verbal and non-verbal—takes place, there is, in addition, a good chance that both Keith and Judy will experience deeper sexual satisfaction than before.

Many of us have been taught that expression of hostility is unloving. On the contrary—anger is always a reality in an alive intimacy. Inviting free exchange allows for the expression of negative feelings. If those feelings are stifled, there will be little expression of positive feelings. What we can do is find less damaging ways of expressing anger.

One important principle we can all learn is not to be defensive when we are confronted. This cannot be overstressed. By not being defensive, we keep channels of communication open. Therefore:

- When confronted by a partner, whether gently or not, listen!
- Say nothing in defense of yourself until you have heard what your mate has to say.
- Absorb it, think it over, and let your intimate know that you have heard what was said.
- Remember that you cannot be destroyed by words, and that even if an accusation is totally correct, you are not a "bad" person. Be slow to judge yourself in a negative light.

Remember, negative feedback is not an attack on your character, regardless of the words used.

Encourage positive change

How can problems be faced openly without damage to either party? When Keith responds to Judy's initial outburst with, "I'm sorry I overlooked calling you." Judy, instead of pouting, can say, "It wasn't really your being late for dinner that made me angry. I guess I'm just afraid that you're getting bored with me." Judy has expressed her feelings without alienating Keith, and he now has the opportunity to deal with her feelings of inadequacy and to encourage her to change without making her feel rejected.

At this point, Keith might say,

- "Perhaps you're feeling bored. Maybe I've been unfair in expecting you to stay home so much."
- "If you'd like to go back to school, we could hire a maid two days a week and I could stay with the kids on the weekends when you need to study. After all, it was partly my fault you dropped out of school in the first place."
- "You always wanted a nursing degree and the training that goes with it. I think you'd make a good nurse!"

The attitude behind such statements reveals insight and awareness on Keith's part. He senses that Judy's need for self-confidence is basic to her communication problem. Without criticizing or rejecting her, he can encourage her self-development. More education and specific training would help Judy reach her potential.

However, if Judy responds to Keith's statements with "You think I'm stupid!" or "You wish you'd married somebody on your own educational level!" or "Why did you insist that we marry anyway?" she is avoiding responsibility to learn.

Develop self-awareness

It can be pointed out here that when one mate accepts a challenge to grow, a whole new assortment of problems may arise. Look at what happens when Judy goes back to school and becomes involved in the nursing program. She begins to gain self-confidence and her friendships and areas of interest broaden.

As a result of her work with patients in the local hospital, she becomes vitally interested in a public health clinic in a poor section of the community. As Keith becomes increasingly aware of Judy's absence from the home, he feels threatened by the depth of her commitment to this new interest. He now realizes that his motives for encouraging change in Judy were mixed. He wanted her to become involved in school, not only for her own sake, but also for his. He wanted to feel more comfortable with their friends, and he wanted her to have work she enjoyed so she would be more understanding and less suspicious when he was busy. He never intended for her work to take her away from the family so much. In addition to his being inconvenienced, he is also genuinely concerned for her safety as she travels to and from work in a slum area. He had not realized that changes in Judy would threaten his own sense of adequacy as a man.

Keith has two options at this point. He can act out his threat, saying, "I'm the man and I'll make the decisions here!" and demand that Judy give up her activities. But a retreat to a male power position to solve a problem would be both archaic and self-defeating. And if Judy gave in to his demand, she would sacrifice personal integrity.

Keith's other option is to recognize the contribution to their relationship of Judy's newfound sense of self-worth, identity, and increasing self-confidence. He can accept his sense of threat and not act on it. Keith can decide to support the growth movements of his spouse, whether he likes the direction they take or not.

Keith realizes that to discourage her would be damaging to their relationship for three reasons: 1) It would be unfair and unfeeling to ask Judy to give up an activity that is emotionally gratifying, intellectually stimulating, and growth-producing. 2) It would make her feel trapped, resentful, and desirous of more freedom from him. 3) It would make him less authentic as a person because his actions would conflict with his words. Because the relationship is more important to him than his own feelings, he prefers to accept her new interest, one in which he is not involved, even though it causes him concern.

While Judy, for the first time, feels she has something extra to give to the relationship, she sees that Keith is also being pushed to grow. Sensing his fear, she realizes that her search for identity and self-development has put a strain on a loving relationship. Therefore, she considers some changes. She joins a car pool, which helps allay her husband's fears when she returns from work after dark. And both of them attempt to take off one afternoon a week to spend time together.

If relationships are to be kept alive, both partners *must grow*. When each supports the growth of the other, each gives up something in exchange; but what they receive in the way of greater caring and mutual growth is beneficial to their relationship.

Intimates Need Growing Mates

Psychologist Carl Rogers recently stated that, through forty years of practice and research in psychotherapy, he had observed that people need a "growing" therapist, not merely a trained one. By the same token, intimates need growing mates who are not afraid to be themselves. The impact of one's personal growth on intimacy cannot be overstressed.

I can personally verify the truth of Rogers' observation. At one point in my life I was a technically competent but not a very dynamic psychotherapist because I was in a rut. My thinking was rigid, "uptight," my opinions too set, and I allowed myself too little personal freedom. After a commitment to my own growth, some group psychotherapy, and several friendships that encouraged growth, I began to change. As a result, I experienced greater acceptance of myself and acceptance of my value to others. I also felt greater self-trust, more confidence in my own decisions, and less concern about social approval. I became more willing to try new things, and even to make mistakes in order to learn. I became, in essence, more my own man.

As a result, my patients began to change more quickly. Some people liked me less; many liked me more. (A clearly defined personality usually does not attract neutral feelings.)

As I changed, my patients changed. More patients came to me who really wanted to change instead of merely wanting to feel more comfortable or to adapt to their surroundings. This happened partially because I did not subtly try to keep them from changing. I think my acceptance of an authentic relationship with persons in psychotherapy released growth forces in me that continue to foster change. And, like my patients, I continue to grow also.

* * *

The illusion inherent in "let me remake you" is that one mate has the right to decide how the other should exist as a person. Yet we know that we do not succeed when we try to be someone we are not. We know that we can be no one as well as we can be ourselves.

The fiction that one's mate can be changed to fit a preconceived image through criticism, pressure, idolatry, or disapproval leads only to the destruction of the relationship. On the other hand, personality in the process of development becomes increasingly individualized, unpredictable, and interesting.

As we apply this knowledge to our relationships with others, especially to our mates, we turn the tables on one of the most destructive fictions about intimacy.

4 | *Write Your Own Intimacy Script*

The illusion that "our parents know best" is destructive and dangerous in intimate relationships—destructive because it prevents us from developing our own patterns, and dangerous because we are largely unaware of it.

Do we really believe that Mother and Father's ways are best? Jean dislikes her mother's tendency to give her father advice, yet she finds herself telling her mate how to live. We behave as if our parents knew best, even though we believe it only marginally at best. The illusion is unconscious and automatic; like a timer set to go off, it is activated almost as soon as the wedding bells ring. The illusion is active in intimate relationships outside of marriage as well.

In an attempt to expose the dangers of this fiction, this chapter examines aspects of intimacy where parental patterns do the most harm. Awareness that these patterns exist is necessary if we wish to modify or change them to fit our here-and-now situation. But the key to change lies not only in knowing, but in acting upon that knowledge by establishing an intimacy that is truly our own. Such an intimacy would be one in which we did not automatically follow 1) the "oughts" and "shoulds" learned at home—and 2) the unexpressed attitudes of the parental script.

Such an intimacy would be founded on patterns which meet our own and our mate's needs.

The Positive Parent

Lest you think we are anti-parent, stop a minute.

Because you may be fortunate enough to have parents who cared for you, in spite of technical child-rearing errors they may have committed, you have a capacity to care for others. When no concerned parent or adult is present during early developmental years, a child does not develop normally; he lags behind emotionally and intellectually and acquires many personality problems.

Positive parent messages, which affirm us, help us maintain a state of well-being and buttress us against the traumas of life. Some of these messages, stated directly and indirectly, convey the following:

- You are a good person.
- You try to do the right thing.
- You are intelligent.
- You are attractive.
- You can make mistakes and learn from them.

We also get from our parents positive messages about behavior, which help us to develop satisfying relationships with others. Such messages are:

- Do be considerate of your spouse.
- Do help with the housework, dishes, etc.
- Do be concerned about grooming, physique, health.
- Do consider your mate's opinion.
- Do show affection.

We would not want to unlearn these messages.

The Negative Parent

Unfortunately, many ideas and behavioral patterns transmitted from parents block intimacy. Before you blame your parents, however, remember that they and their parents did not have the science of psychology available to them. Many of the treatment techniques developed by modern psychiatry and psychology were not practiced or publicized in our parents' day.

Some of the more damaging parent messages that work unconsciously are these:

- Do not get close.
- Do not be open.
- Do not show emotion.
- Do not show affection.
- Do not express negative feelings.

It is easy to see what the practice of these messages does to intimacy.

Most people do not perceive the messages directly. But they may discover them in other ways:

—listening to descriptions of their relationships in review (cold or warm, distant or close, guarded or open);
—discovering how others (therapy group members, therapist, friends, spouse) see them.

For example, in a recent session of patients using audiovisual playback to study non-verbal behavior, one patient discussed his awareness that he tended to use humor with barbs to keep people at a distance, even though he wanted to be closer. Some of the group experienced him as speaking from a great emotional distance. Others said they wished to get close to him but would not risk it, fearing a verbal jab. Several group members experienced the feeling that they were about to establish a close relationship, but never quite made it. This feeling kept them trying to get closer.

With two television cameras focused on the group, and with one camera showing close-up expressions of the therapists, the playback on two television screens was meaningful. The sheer pleasure on the person's face as he made his humorous barbs was impossible to deny. He reflected an obvious feeling of control as the others experienced "almost getting close" to him.

After several years of psychotherapy, he had worked hard to rid himself of parental prohibitions which said: "Do not get close." Even then, he still needed feedback to correct behavior originating from parent messages.

Do we ever reach the point where we do not need to check out how we are seen by others? Not if personality growth is to continue.

Normal Separation from Parents

Post-Freudian psychology has stressed that personality growth can continue throughout life. Although basic personality patterns are established by age six, changes do continue to occur. These changes may be more profound at certain periods in our lives.

For example, a major change occurs during adolescence, when a youngster enters into the normal process of reevaluating his place within family relationships. A basic developmental task of adolescence is to establish identity as a female or male person, separate from one's parents. Adolescent rebellion is a positive push for more independence, a struggle to achieve a sense of personal identity. In some cultures, adolescent rebellion is virtually unknown, because puberty rites introduce a child to the adult world, or because there is an opportunity to experience adult roles within socially defined limits. Rebellion in our society, where no formal rites exist, would be less likely to mushroom if adolescents were encouraged before puberty to know themselves and to develop their own view of life. Children are not only inadequately prepared for emotional independence during the first ten years of life, but rarely successfully achieve it by the end of adolescence.

Psychological separation from parents may be painful to both generations, but it is essential if the teenager is to learn to do his own thinking, establish a value system which has personal meaning, and assume responsibility for his own life. In an atmosphere of freedom within realistic limits, he can accept some and reject other parental patterns he has learned and observed as a child. The extent to which he is aware which aspects of his family culture will best meet his needs will determine the extent to which he is able to form a new and different family culture for himself.

Many adults have difficulty forming their own culture. Because of inadequate separation from parents, they are placed in the difficult position of living in two family groups simultaneously. Sometimes the fact that parents are so helpful during emotional or financial crises keeps offspring over-involved at the expense of self-sufficiency. Sometimes a son or daughter may not wish to separate from parents. Either way, one cannot be a full partner to an intimacy when he or she is attached to Mother's apron strings or Dad's wallet.

Parental Patterns That Affect Intimacy

Natural stages of personality development allow for the sorting out of parental patterns, with some being kept, others discarded. However, rarely do we systematically reevaluate family patterns in areas crucial to intimacy.

The two areas most seriously affected in intimacy are those which involve expression of caring, and patterns of dominance vs. submissiveness. Awareness of how parental patterns in these areas control us is essential to understanding a variety of problems of intimacy.

Expression of Caring

Caring is expressed overtly in three basic ways:

- physical contact;
- words;
- deeds.

You may feel comfortable with one style of expressing caring because it is one your family used. In the case of Martha and Ted, differences in the ways caring was expressed—ways which were learned from parents—affected their intimacy profoundly. Martha's parents rarely showed any physical affection and seldom expressed fond feelings in words. Instead, they demonstrated concern for other members of the family by a conscientious pursuit of household activities. Mother was remembered as always being busy in the kitchen, ironing clothes, and washing dishes, while Father was responsible for yard work, household repairs, and family recreation. In Ted's family there was much open display of warmth and affection, accompanied by a somewhat casual approach to work around the house. His parents expressed caring physically, while Martha's expressed it through their actions. Neither set of parents verbalized caring to any degree.

The interaction of these two markedly different family patterns created an intense marital problem. Ted felt rejected because Martha did not drop her work to give him an affectionate embrace when he arrived home, whereas Martha felt rejected because Ted "did not care enough" to do what needed to be done in the yard or house.

When Ted and Martha began to work on their problem, they rated themselves and their parents on how caring was expressed by words, deeds, and touch. Their patterns are plotted on the three continuums shown on the following page.

If you wish to rate yourself and your parents on patterns of caring, make a continuum like the one preceding. Discuss your self-rating with your mate to correct misperceptions. Occasionally two persons have different ideas about where on the continuum each falls. You may perceive that your score is average, while your mate may feel that your score is below average in a particular area. Just spotting the differences in expectations of what is average is a start toward changes that can help both persons.

It is important that decisions to change be mutual. Attempts to force another person to change before there is readiness may only retard progress.

Touching More

If both of you want changes toward more expression of physical affection, practice touching each other more. At first, you may feel stiff and awkward, but that will change once you have decided definitely how you wish to express affection. You can learn to touch more by degrees, by

- hand-holding, patting—
- arm-clasping or holding—
- caressing and embracing—
- petting as a prelude to intercourse—
- prolonged sexual intercourse.

TED AND MARTHA:

TWO GENERATIONS OF THE EXPRESSION OF CARING

1. PHYSICAL AFFECTION (TOUCH)

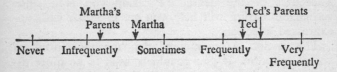

2. VERBAL AFFECTION (WORDS)

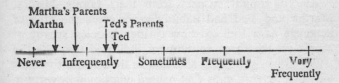

3. ACTIONS PERFORMED (DEEDS)

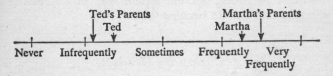

Verbalizing Caring

Caring may be expressed by statements which vary in emotional distance according to choice of words. "I love you," for example, is usually more personal than "You're a love." Word choice and voice tone communicate varying degrees of endearment and feeling. Of course, all such expressions are personal, and knowing the individual is the key to knowing the depth of affection conveyed by each expression.

When you compare your use of verbal affection with your parents', you might perceive a need to increase your use of spoken affection. If so, you can begin to work at it now. Progressing from "infrequently" to "frequently" on the continuum will result in a greater awareness of the degree of caring you feel, since verbalizing caring will help you get in touch with unexpressed affection.

This is not to recommend the "mechanization" of verbal affection. If you genuinely wish to be more affectionate and a reservoir of affection for the other person already exists, an increase in spoken affection is an authentic change.

As you might suspect from their family history, Martha and Ted had habitually neglected the area of language as a tool to show caring. A quick survey of scores on the three continuums indicated that Martha and Ted were showing affection as their respective parents did, leaving gaps that caused emotional poverty in their relationship. As both worked on changing their patterns, both experienced greater satisfaction in moving toward a balanced, yet integrated, way of expressing affection that was to become "their" way.

Caring by Deeds

There is no automatic relationship between caring and action. Because we live by meaning, acts express caring only when they are meaningful to the recipient. For example, a husband may be sincerely convinced that working seventy hours a week is the supreme way to show concern for his family's welfare, while the simple act of picking up a loaf of bread on the way home means more to his wife than the extra dollars. It is her meaning system that determines whether his act shows caring.

By discussing which actions mean caring to us, we can, like Martha and Ted, learn to act in ways that express the caring that really exists with an intimate.

As they worked on all three means of communicating affection, Martha and Ted found themselves making more consistent attempts to please than be pleased. A better person-to-person relationship developed, relatively free of ideas about how the other "should" act. This meant changing from a parental injunction, "It should be this way," to a personal inquiry, "What is our way?" With such changes, the relationship became more conducive to personality growth and the satisfaction of mutual needs.

Is it realistic to act out a family pattern at the expense of creating a satisfying relationship for ourselves here and now? Ask yourself two questions:

- Is my style of expressing caring working well in my relationship?
- Is my pattern a conscious choice on my part?

Exercising Power in Intimacy

Another important aspect of intimacy, patterned after parents, is that of dominance versus submissiveness.

Let's take the case of Ted and Martha, which is plotted on the following dominant-submissive continuum. The key explains the positions of Martha, Martha's parents, Ted, and Ted's parents.

The diagram depicts Martha and Ted as about equal partners, and each more dominant than submissive in their relationship. Does something have to give? No; since "power" is shared, collaboration takes place. Both partners are strong, and a dominant/submissive dichotomy is avoided.

Martha actually admires her father. She feels sorry for her mother and does not choose to be as passive. Happily for her own relationship, she does not over-

TED AND MARTHA:
TWO GENERATIONS OF POWER DISTRIBUTION

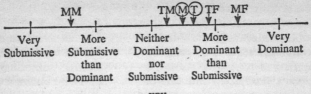

Very Submissive	More Submissive than Dominant	Neither Dominant nor Submissive	More Dominant than Submissive	Very Dominant

KEY

Ⓜ = Martha   MM = Martha's Mother   TM = Ted's Mother
Ⓣ = Ted   MF = Martha's Father   TF = Ted's Father

identify with her father's power tactics. She chose a man who required neither a submissive nor a dominant mate. As a result, their relationship is more or less free of parental power patterns which would interfere with the growth of both partners.

The following diagram of another husband (X), however, shows a problem situation of a dominant mother, passive father, and a mate (Y) who assumes a very submissive role.

TWO GENERATIONS OF POWER

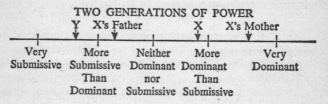

Very Submissive	More Submissive Than Dominant	Neither Dominant nor Submissive	More Dominant Than Submissive	Very Dominant

The husband-wife relationship here fits conventional, although outdated, ideas of power distribution by sex. There is little to recommend this degree of dominance imbalance.

When there is a tendency for a mother to be dominant in the parental relationship, as reflected in this diagram, the son may be unusually alert to any dominant traits in his wife. He may overreact and suppress normal assertive trends by his wife, even though he allowed them during their courtship days. Assertive trends within marriage become a serious threat to him, since he does not wish to find himself in the submissive role assumed by his father.

Psychotherapy, or open discussion between X and Y, can help them see the gains of a more equal distribution of dominance. As X realizes his mate is very unlike his mother, and will not become similar, he can encourage less submissiveness. Actually, Y only wants to be average, and is agreeable to having X slightly more dominant.

When one parent, whether mother or father, is markedly dominant, the idea of shared power is rarely learned. Nevertheless, recognition of personality differences between one's parents and oneself can help alter patterns that do not fit the present intimacy situation.

Discussion of differences might be the basis for a decision to change.

You and your intimate may wish to discuss how you see yourselves in relationship to parents in the area of submissiveness and dominance. Visualize a continuum with as many positions between extremes as you wish. Drawing a continuum like the examples in this chapter may help you specify differences.

If you are not happy with what you learn, remember: One gestalt psychotherapy principle for changing behavior is to experiment. Don't be afraid to try new patterns. If a submissive female can try to be more assertive, and her mate can work to counter built-in fear of female domination, or vice-versa, change beneficial to both can occur.

Control vs. Dominance

It is often assumed, incorrectly, that dominance and control are synonymous. Actually, the more passive member of a pair may exercise greater control in the relationship. A mate who withholds information or affection may exercise considerable control, even if he or she is quite passive. This is especially true if the more dominant mate makes most of the overtures, takes most of the risks. Of course, control only for the sake of power is self-defeating, for what good is control without gratification in the relationship?

A dominance struggle is becoming commonplace in relationships today as women increase their demands for status. But even where conflict does not take place openly, quiet rivalry may occur where each person tries to outdo the other. Power struggles often emerge before the couple has had time to develop a sense of unity.

The achievement of more equal status between men and women actually paves the way for genuine collaboration instead of increased competition. When there is collaboration, the accomplishments and skills of each are seen not only as reflecting well on the other, but also as contributing to each's sense of fulfillment. Both men and women "win" when neither dominates the other.

How can a person get in touch with patterns of control in intimacy? Experiment with your own control patterns by trying an exercise used in group therapy.

Couples pair off (either marital pairs or male and female members of a group), and join hands facing each other. The exercise is non-verbal; no words may be spoken. Whoever decides to move first takes command. With hands always joined, one person leads the other any way desired for a predetermined length of time (about five minutes). Then the control shifts, and the follower leads. When the exercise is over, both persons discuss their feelings about controlling and being controlled.

Usually women either "hand over" control to men at first, or men think they should lead. Some men feel "ladies should be first" and wait out their partners. Avoidance of taking control, or evidence of a wish to control, is transparent with the exercise.

Some persons lead very vigorously, having their partner turn, twist, or even be pressed to the floor.

Others lead gingerly, afraid to offend or be too rough. Some partners move very gracefully together, as if in a dance, and there is little change with the shift of control. These patterns reveal underlying personality tendencies to control or be controlled, and how control is exercised in a relationship.

We have tried to help you work through the fiction that "our parents know best" with greater awareness of how you have been influenced in the giving and receiving of affection as well as dominant/submissive patterns in intimacy. Change will take place only with steady efforts to translate awareness into action.

Other areas of intimacy that are heavily influenced by parental training and example are approached as questions in the next section. Remember: A conscious decision to change in your own direction mobilizes forces to create your own lifestyle.

Like or Unlike Parents?

BUDGET

What does money mean to you?

What do you spend money for?

FRIENDS

What kind of people do you like?

How do you greet people?

Do you like to entertain frequently?

APPEARANCE

Do you prefer "mod" styles or is your taste conservative?

How important is overall appearance to you?

Will weight gain or loss threaten you?

Will aging make you unhappy?

SEPARATENESS

To what extent can you allow autonomy? privacy? separate interests? separate friends?

VALUES

What are your basic ethical values?

To what do you give priority: work? family? money? aesthetics? friends?

RELIGION

Are your religious views conservative or liberal?

How important to you are your beliefs?

How do you feel about taking, or sending, the children to church or synagogue?

CHILD-REARING

How many children do you want?

Who should handle the discipline? how much? what kind?

Do you favor modern or traditional approaches to child-rearing?

SEX ROLES

How do you see male and female roles?

What specific functions are masculine? feminine?

How do you expect a male and female to exercise leadership? show affection?

Once intimates have decided where they stand on these questions in relation to parents, genuine individual differences between mates become apparent. Once they are out in the open, these differences can be largely reconciled to create a pattern which is original with them.

* * *

Open decisions about differences between intimates and their parents, and about individual differences between mates, will pave the way for making decisions that suit you as a twosome. Adherence to the illusion that your parents' way is best will not only obscure your choice to form your own culture, but will also tend to lead you into the "no-change" relationship of which O'Neill's *Open Marriage* speaks. This relationship is one which eventually ends in stagnation, since choices are based on hypothetical social norms.

Awareness of original family patterns, as well as awareness of new options for intimacy, allow us to exercise choices in ways that encourage growth. Acceptance of the uniqueness of each intimacy, plus the recognition that there are many options available, is a step toward ending the illusion that our parents' way is best for us. Ending this illusion means increasing the pleasure of our intimacy.

5 | Divorce Without Failure Is a Chance for Success

DIVORCE.

The word flashes across the minds of many like a bright neon sign blinking "failure . . . failure . . . failure . . ." People considering a divorce seem to envision a scarlet "D" stamped across all personal records and relationships. Dreading public and private censure, they refuse to consider divorce as an option.

Perhaps the true failure in divorce is our failure to see it as a realistic and acceptable solution to the problem of an intimate relationship which no longer satisfies the individuals involved. Whether marital problems stem from unrealistic expectations, poor mate selection initially, or personal growth differences, divorce is a viable alternative which is often ignored because of social taboos.

Where did we get the idea that intimacy, in or out of marriage, is supposed to be happy forever (with the same person)? The assumption is that if we only knew what to do and could avoid mistakes, divorce would never happen. But intimacy itself involves risk, and we are never guaranteed a happy ending.

Even if we make serious mistakes which contribute heavily to termination of a relationship, divorce does not brand us failures as persons. When we are able to accept the idea that marriages are not made in heaven, we will see that divorce is a realistic alternative here on earth. From such a perspective, divorce becomes not failure but an opportunity to find gratifying intimacy, end a frustrating relationship, and continue personal growth in a better situation.

Excuses for Avoiding Divorce

Let's look at some typical excuses people use to explain staying in unhappy marriages, and some possible responses:

EXCUSE: I don't consider divorce an option, since I agreed to take the bad with the good.

ANSWER: You trap yourself when you eliminate divorce as an option.

EXCUSE: There has never been a divorce in my family, and I don't want to be the black sheep.

ANSWER: You can choose to be an example to your family of a person who will not settle for an unhappy marriage.

EXCUSE: Let's face it. I don't want to admit to myself or others that I have failed to make my marriage work.

ANSWER: You know, though, if your marriage is not what you need, and others are rarely fooled by a pretense of happiness.

EXCUSE: I would rather stay married and make the best of it than face the humiliation and embarrassment of divorce.

ANSWER: Your choice, of course. But any embarrassment you feel may be a small price to pay for future years of successful living.

EXCUSE: I don't want my children to live with our failure to have a satisfying marriage.

ANSWER: Your children *are* living with your unhappy marriage, and with all the destructive effects that living with unhappiness can have on them.

EXCUSE: I don't believe I can build a new life and be happy after the problems of a divorce.

ANSWER: Divorce provides an opportunity to find satisfaction when it has been missing, and sharpens an appreciation of a gratifying relationship.

EXCUSE: Our problems have gone on so long, and we have worked so hard on our marriage, that it seems a pity to end our efforts in divorce.

ANSWER: There is sadness, yes. But if you have made unsuccessful efforts to resolve marital problems, divorce may be a successful solution to your problems.

The destructive bite of the illusion that divorce is evidence of personal failure reaches out in several directions, causing people to

- feel guilty about divorce.
- stay in a marriage for the wrong reasons.
- deny themselves and their partner the opportunity to achieve happiness elsewhere.
- measure marital success by whether they stay together.

A sense of pride derived from staying in a marriage that is a miserable experience for one or both may be the biggest mistake of all. Are you really being responsible for yourself when you allow a state of intimacy deprivation to continue? Fortunately, the law is beginning to respond to knowledge of human relations with changes in divorce proceedings.

The Law Does Not Require a Villain

Divorce is a legal act to end a marriage contract. That contract is a public record of two people's agreement to live together and be bound by the marriage laws of their state. In several states, divorce may now take place legally without blame being placed on either partner. The change in language is evidence of a change in attitude. The courts now recognize that divorce need not be evidence of wrongdoing or personal failure by either partner. "Incompatibility"—the reality that two people no longer want to live together as husband and wife because of individual differences—is now an accepted reason for divorce. Evidence of "mental cruelty," adultery, or other acts is no longer necessary to justify the split in some states.

Guilt feelings about a divorce are an albatross around the neck of many divorcées who deserve to think better of themselves. Instead of feeling affirmed by the courage to take a stand for a satisfying intimacy by divorcing, they are nagged by self-doubts that whisper, "If only I had tried this or that, the relationship might have worked."

Regardless of efforts to make a relationship work, some do not. This is not to say that the marriage was never a satisfying one. A marriage may work well for a couple at one point in their lives, but be a mistake at a later stage.

Is it realistic to expect couples to be happily married for three or four decades?

Perhaps with increasing awareness of ourselves and others, the probability will increase that intimates can stay together happily for several decades. However, one might be just as happy with someone else and experience greater growth as well. Perhaps in the future a new expectation will emerge that even very satisfying relationships will terminate within ten years. A relationship that is satisfying this year may not be satisfying in five years because people and relationships change. In fact, healthy people and relationships change often.

Divorce as a New Start

Divorce, on the other hand, is no panacea for marital problems. A new start usually entails dealing with some problems from the past. Several realities can take the starch out of a new life:

- bittersweet memories;
- children of the former union;
- child support and/or alimony payments;
- behavior patterns that lead to making the same mistake twice.

Of these realities, repeating problem patterns is perhaps the most formidable obstacle on the path to improved intimacy in a new relationship. Often a person is unaware that a problem is being repeated. If the tendency to continue in problem patterns is not changed, divorce cannot be the door to enjoyable intimacy.

Some patterns people fall into are these:

- one-sided relationships:
- the search for an opposite;
- self-alienation;
- lack of involvement.

A one-sided relationship

Virginia, at thirty-four, recently divorced, is going with a man of forty and is considering her second marriage. She wants to check out her choice and see if it is sound from an objective, third-party point of view. Initial interviews indicate that Virginia is a bright, attractive person, who has an enthusiasm for living. She is independent and makes few demands on others. She is able to win the confidence and trust of persons usually guarded and suspicious, and her relationships with both males and females are excellent—except for one consistent pattern. She assumes a helping role with friends.

You may wonder why this should be a problem.

Her first husband, although highly intelligent, trusted almost no one, and had no really close relationships. He gave little emotionally or sexually, and depended on Virginia to harmonize family relationships with their two children.

She gave to him until she decided that her morale and motivation were so low that something had to be done. Her husband refused psychotherapy, and made no effort to correct his pattern of non-giving. Her decision to divorce ushered in a period of contentment and peace of mind she had not experienced since marriage. No longer was she subject to the put-downs of a husband.

A year later, she met a lawyer, also divorced, who treated her with consideration. No doubt he loved her, but it was apparent that Virginia was supplying about 80 percent of the emotional and intellectual stimulation in the relationship. On the surface, he appeared quite different from her first husband, but he also would not allow anyone to get close to him. Virginia maintained an intimacy with him by a steadfast effort to relax his defenses, and poured abundant emotional warmth into the relationship. She failed to see that she was repeating an old pattern of being more of a "giver" than a "receiver," and thereby denying herself the satisfaction of a truly mutual relationship.

Another blind spot which prevented insight was Virginia's tendency to look at the bright side of life. She saw the positive aspects of a person to the exclusion of everything else. This tendency, while helpful in establishing relationships with difficult personalities, needed to be balanced with a realistic appraisal of negative aspects of the relationship. Then the intimacy would be healthy for both persons.

Psychotherapy helped Virginia see areas of herself which she had previously screened out, and focused attention on her tendency to allow destructive patterns to develop in intimate relationships. She felt cheated when this happened, but seemed powerless to change. After she recognized the payoff she received by feeling needed, and feeling secure because she did not need much, she decided the rewards were not worth it. She asked her fiancé to give more of himself by supporting her emotionally, responding to her as a person, being attentive to her needs, and showing affection. When he either did not or could not respond in a more giving manner, she ended the relationship and avoided a repeat of her previous marriage.

Is it frightening to you how easily Virginia was repeating an old pattern which guaranteed intimacy deprivation?

Virginia's problem is not an uncommon one. Many people, especially those in "helping" professions (medicine, social work, psychology, and education), are attracted to relationships where they help the intimate. A need to give may be one reason they enter such professions in the first place. But a good intimate relationship must be mutual.

After several sessions over a space of five months, Virginia was able to change her pattern by selecting men who could form a give-and-take relationship. Long-term psychotherapy was not needed, since she began to pay close attention to how much a man gave to her in a relationship.

She now has a satisfying relationship with a man who is very warm and responsive. At first she felt insecure receiving as much as she gave, and somewhat insecure because he appeared more self-sufficient, and less in need, than past males in her life. But the new rewards of intimacy have more than offset the self-defeating payoff of security received as a "giver."

If your intimacy is not a satisfying one, why not check it out with a psychotherapist to determine the problem? If you have car trouble, you take it to a mechanic, and for safekeeping have a checkup every ten thousand miles. Do you feel inadequate because you are not an expert with cars? Personal relationships are far more complex, yet we hesitate, or find reasons to avoid, seeing a professional psychologist. But the average practitioner can identify patterns like Virginia's in a few sessions. After diagnosis, such problems can be worked on alone, or with professional help.

The "opposites attract" mix-up

The idea that someone who is the opposite from one-self is attractive may create a problem that is rarely solved by ending a relationship. For example, a person who is independent and assertive will overtly desire to have a dependent, passive partner, and selects an individual who fits the part. He or she then becomes increasingly dissatisfied because the mate is not able to maintain a share of responsibilities. This resentment places the passive partner in a conflict situation where, in order to be attractive, he or she must be not only passive and compliant, but also somehow assertive, confident, and autonomous. Finding it impossible to meet these conflicting needs, the passive mate will experience little acceptance from the intimate.

Solving a problem like this by divorce makes it possible for the aggressive partner to find another mate who fits the same passive, compliant role, and who will also be trapped in the same neurotic relationship where genuine acceptance is not possible.

Mr. and Mrs. M are an extreme case. Each had a previous marital partner who had been diagnosed as schizophrenic. Because their former mates had been hospitalized as hopelessly psychotic with little chance for recovery, Mr. and Mrs. M were relieved of a sense of responsibility for their divorces.

Freed from responsibility and without the benefit of psychological or psychiatric therapy, they selected each other as marriage companions. When their marriage began to show serious signs of deterioration, a careful diagnosis was made of their personalities and interpersonal patterns, and it was not difficult to see how they might have contributed to the mental illness of their marriage partners.

First, they appeared to choose people who had strong tendencies to become disturbed. Second, each would push the mate to a "breaking point." Although in relationships outside of marriage both husband and wife demonstrated good will toward others, in close, sustained relationships they clearly manifested destructive patterns. Each would use what he or she knew about the other's weaknesses to push the other to a point of no return. Mr. M would work day and night, refuse sex, accuse his wife of "being crazy," attack her self-esteem, and lose his temper and shout. Mrs. M would scream for attention, tell him how inadequate he was as a lover and husband, and ask for things he could not give, such as happiness.

A major consideration in working with this problem was to prevent the couple from divorcing prematurely and transmitting the problems of each other into other relationships. The first task was to prevent one or the other from driving the partner crazy. The second was to produce enough personality change so that they would not need to maintain a relationship wherein one partner was weak and the other seemingly strong.

It was important to be able to counsel them as a crisis emerged, in order to nip it in the bud. On one occasion when the husband threatened to "put his wife in the hospital" it was necessary to go to their home and talk to them. Both of them were alienated from their true feelings, and some time passed before their feelings of being threatened, rejected, and afraid of becoming insane surfaced. When efforts to "drive the other person crazy" were pointed out, some of the destructive behavior was abandoned. They did choose to continue living together, and eventually gained some insight into their problems.

A happy ending? I doubt it. However, a divorce in this case might not have led to better intimacy for either person.

Self-alienation: A contemporary problem

Continual damage to self-esteem, even though not coming from a mate, may lead to divorce. The alienated partner feels unable to become the person he or she wants to be in the marriage, and is frustrated by feelings of irritation and dissatisfaction.

Roy, twenty-eight years old and the son of a successful real-estate developer, was six months into a second marriage. He wanted to be caring and understanding, but seemed irritable, negative, and dissatisfied. During his first marriage he had placed the blame for his dissatisfaction on his mate.

It was a major step when he realized that the focus of his problem was the way he treated himself. He was a perfectionist, hard on himself, and out of touch with his feelings—all of which led to self-alienation. After a time in psychotherapy, Roy began to see that he was trying to earn love like the moralist, by "doing everything right." When he fell short of his impossibly high standards, he disliked himself and felt others disliked him, too. As Roy began to accept his humanness, he began to like himself better. He was then able to receive love as a gift.

If he had not looked within himself for the roots of his dissatisfaction, he might have continued to place the blame on his mate. Divorce would then have been another expression of his not being in touch with the human side of himself.

Lack of involvement

In some cases, a couple heads toward divorce because primary involvements develop outside of the marriage. Each person reacts to the outside involvements of the other by extending his own involvements until the fires of warmth have been extinguished. Then little effort is invested in keeping the relationship alive.

SHE: We hardly sleep together anymore, because he is often away on business trips.

HE: She has her club activities, so she has little need or time for me.

She: He has several friendships which I don't share,
and I have mine.

He: We don't have much to say to each other.

These mates live separate lives and meet intimacy
needs with other persons. Very little happens between
them, not even quarrels. If one of the mates wants a
deeper personal involvement in marriage, and the other
is willing to settle for appearances, something has to
give.

A lack of involvement in some marriages is tanta-
mount to emotional divorce without legal action. When
two people stop talking, avoid each other, or talk only
about the business side of the relationship, emotional
divorce is on the way. Unless some effort is made to
communicate, there is no way to tell whether involvement in the marriage can be revived. Some painful emotions often surface if communication starts, but a
renewal of active caring may help to heal the pain of
old hurts brought to the surface. Remember, even pain
is more meaningful than an absence of feelings. If
nothing can be revived in the relationship, divorce is a
humane solution, unless both persons wish to coexist.

Protest Against Old Marriage Models

As society passes through dramatic and dynamic
changes and taxes individual resources for adaptation
to change, the marriage models of the past seem inadequate for the present. In contrast to the past, when
husbands or wives just gritted their teeth in unhappy
marriages and "made the best of it," today fewer are
willing to tolerate the absence of fulfilling intimacy in
a close relationship.

Placing the blame on marriage may be a way to
avoid problems within ourselves. Still, a marriage model
which is not flexible enough to allow for individual differences and outside friendships will stagnate and stunt
the growth of the participants.

Nena and George O'Neill,
For Couples (New York: M. Evans & Co., 1972), p. 74.

Open Marriage describes marriages as either "open" or "closed," according to the psychological contract under which a couple lives. These contracts look like this:

Closed Contract	*Open Contract*
Ownership of the mate	Undependent living
Denial of self	Personal growth
Playing the couples game	Individual freedom
Rigid role behavior	Flexible roles
Absolute fidelity	Mutual trust
Total exclusivity	Expansion through openness*

A truly open marriage, if it worked for a couple, might prevent divorce, since the absence of rigid restrictions would allow each person space for personal growth within the framework of marriage. But because we have been conditioned to "closed marriage," the open marriage contract may seem idealistic. Few marriages are entirely open or closed. In every marriage there are some areas where more openness may be applied; in other areas neither person may want more openness. A marriage floundering on the verge of divorce might not be helped by an open contract. At any rate, couples have the option to talk over the open contract and see where agreement can be reached about change. After all, *movement toward* more openness in marriage is what matters.

New models within marriage are also developing. A recent article in a woman's magazine spelled out a specific legal contract between a man and woman married by public record. They left little to chance about where they stood with each other. Details about religion, outside relationships, children, separate careers, care and use of living space, property, debts, and deci-

* Nena and George O'Neill, *Open Marriage: A New Life Style for Couples* (New York: M. Evans & Co., 1972), p. 74.

sion-making were worked out, defined, and subject to annual review for purposes of change. A commitment was made to seek professional help from a third party should problems arise or portions of the contract be broken.

The courts of each state determine the marriage laws of that state. In the case of individually written contracts such as the one just mentioned, the contract has the value of helping a couple decide on major issues before marriage.

I recommend that every couple, *before* they marry, discuss how problems should be approached and, if divorce is eventually chosen, how this will take place. Every business partnership spells out how each partner may leave the arrangement, so that later disagreement may be avoided. The time to reach an amicable agreement on termination of a relationship is at the beginning, not at the end, of one.

This may sound cold-blooded, but the emotional pain and suffering experienced when termination is *not* discussed, and divorce occurs, pleads for a solution. Most relationships which terminate would end on a much better note, and perhaps be maintained in a new form, if problems with termination were solved. It may be more often the rule than the exception that even good intimate relationships will have to end in time if growth and satisfaction are to be sustained in our lives.

Marital Martyrdom

How much abuse should one take from a mate before deciding on a divorce?

One patient showed extreme courage in the face of psychologically brutal treatment (untrue accusations) from a mentally ill mate. This woman, understanding her husband's thought distortions, was able to excel in community activities, fulfill adequately her role as wife and mother, and achieve the satisfaction of seeing her children grow up and go off to college without subjecting them to financial hardship. As much as possible, she protected her children from the marital discord and the torrent of abuse she had learned to take.

Several professionals who had been called in on the case could offer no hope of resolution of the problem, yet it was her decision to continue the marriage until permanent hospitalization of the mate was necessary.

Is such marital courage, where change doesn't seem possible, fair to oneself? There are two sides to the question, but only the persons involved can decide. All too often friends, relatives, and even professional counselors subtly usurp the rights of individuals to make their own decisions, trying to decide for them how much they should take in a marriage. They forget that no one can abide by someone else's decision.

Hopefully, the person who is being a martyr will look at the marriage from several points of view, and ask these questions.

- How well as I coping with emotional pain and deprivation in the relationship?
- How would I feel if divorce were chosen?
- How would each offspring be affected?
- What are the financial consequences of divorce?
- What am I saying to my children by staying in the marriage?
- Am I aware of what needs of mine are not being met?

The answer to the question "Should I divorce?" may emerge naturally as a person answers the above questions.

What About Children?

A decision to divorce, no matter how self-directed, is not made in a vacuum. At least one other person is affected, more if there are children.

If child-rearing is a major value for a couple, the effects of divorce on children is a major issue. Let's examine the pros and cons of divorce on children.

The "Cons" (negative effects)

- Divorce cannot end the strong biological and psychological tie to a parent. It is painful for a child to be separated from a parent for any reason.
- If the mother keeps the children, a son loses the proximity of the primary male in his life, and a daughter loses the presence of her first male attachment, which sets a precedent for all other male relationships.
- A child may be left, after divorce, with a disturbed parent, increasing the probability that the child may become disturbed. One healthy parent can generally counteract an unhealthy one.
- Divided loyalty in divorce can create severe inner conflict for a child.
- Divorce ordinarily means at least temporary financial insecurity for a child (perhaps the loss of money for a college education, for example).

The "Pros" (positive effects)

- A deprived intimacy teaches a child how *not* to be intimate—the wrong lesson. Divorce opens the door to new intimacies for both persons.
- Children may become the focus of marital problems, bearing the brunt of hostilities. Divorce can be an end to conflict which can cause emotional problems in children.
- A husband's or wife's performance as a parent is impaired if a marriage relationship is disturbing. Divorce may remove tensions which obstruct effective parent-child relations.

- A child can maintain a relationship with each parent following divorce, in an atmosphere which is conflict-free.
- In many cases a stepfather or stepmother provides an additional model after whom the child may pattern his behavior.

Each family situation is different. The emotional status of each parent and of individual children, as well as the coping ability of a parent who would have custody following divorce, are important to consider.

A complex situation? Yes, but most people have the ability to think objectively enough to assess the effects of a divorce on their children.

Everyone Can Afford Some Help

If a divorce is being considered, I would recommend at least one to three sessions with a trained psychotherapist to help couples, or individuals, evaluate their situation.

You may be willing to see a professional but think you can't afford it. Long-term psychotherapy does add up to a major expense, but a few sessions to help you evaluate your situation may actually save you money. Divorce alone is costly, and a professional may help you work out your problems.

Licensed psychologists, or psychiatrists, and certified social workers are available in private practice for professional help. In addition, many communities have guidance clinics or family counseling agencies available whose fees are adjusted to income.

* * *

Whatever your choice may be, remember that divorce does not mean failure. Divorce is a major tool for putting an end to intimacy deprivation in our lives and for allowing us the chance to find satisfying intimate relationships.

A valuable option indeed!

6 | We Should Expect Respect, Honesty, and Forgiveness in Intimacy

Underlying the fiction that "marriage will make me happy" is the idea that marriage, by some magic, will solve all our personal problems and meet all our needs. This fiction places an oppressive burden on one's mate and robs the relationship—and its participants—of potential joy.

A young wife experiences creeping unhappiness after six months of marriage. After two years of college, she had quit school, married, and moved into an apartment with her husband, a recently graduated engineer. She had accepted the idea that, as if by magic, marriage to the right person would equal satisfaction in life. As a result, she blames herself for feeling discontented, since her husband is a "good provider, fun to be with, and a fine person." Neither parents, friends, nor the educational system had told her that her mate alone would not satisfy all her needs.

Everyone has psychological needs for recognition, approval, security, belonging, and growth—needs which may be partially met in marriage. But while husbands and wives may contribute to their partner's sense of well-being, no one has the power to create happiness for another.

All too often, the sense of fun enjoyed before the

marriage seems to be replaced by a growing disappointment, which is usually the result of the unrealistic expectation that marriage alone can make you happy.

The fiction is usually accompanied by expectations of what each mate should contribute to marriage. These expectations are self-imposed and form the basis for a series of demands which grows until the essential joy of the relationship is snuffed out under a wet blanket of obligations.

As areas of dissatisfaction develop, ideas of what each partner "deserves" for happiness may balloon out of proportion: "I am unhappy because you are not keeping the house clean, cooking what I like, disciplining the children correctly, staying home more, improving your mind," and so on. Disappointed expectations spread to all areas of the relationship, causing emotional pain. As hurt and disappointment make loving appear dangerous, the relationship becomes a breeding ground for antagonism and resentment.

Resentment, which is usually a defense against being hurt, seems a "safer" way to relate, since one may feel less vulnerable and more protected while being resentful. Yet resentment as a major way of relating is ugly. This sequence—from feeling disappointed, to feeling vulnerable, to being resentful—creates a situation where happiness cannot exist.

Where does a belief in magic begin in the first place? The idea that any "magic," marital or otherwise, will make us happy originates in childhood and is perpetuated by fairy tales where people live "happily ever after" without turmoil. Actually, the belief in magic dies hard in adults. Time after time, intelligent, successful adults are seen in psychotherapists' offices still captured by the belief that some magic will occur to make their lives OK if only they are patient and wait long enough for the magic to happen.

Even trained psychotherapists have trouble sometimes with their inner child's belief in magic. Once a successful and prominent psychotherapist presented to a training group of mental health professionals his problem of being too passive. The leader of the training group, using a combination of transactional analysis and gestalt psychotherapy techniques, asked the person to picture himself as a child, which he did. He visualized himself in a scene at his childhood home, sitting alone as an eight-year-old boy. Speaking for the eight-year-old part of himself, he expressed feelings of loneliness and inability to do anything about it. He also made contact with the feeling that, if he waited long enough, some magic would occur to solve his problem. (As a child, he perceived that he could not act to change his situation.)

He was asked to visualize himself saying "goodbye" to the image of himself as a relatively helpless, passive child who was waiting for magic.

He did this in a poignant scene which brought tears to his eyes, and which also touched the other group members. After actually waving goodbye to the part of himself waiting for magic to change things, he faced the sadness of separation from a facet of himself carried over from childhood. He then decided, as an adult, to commit himself to being more assertive in relationships.

Although major changes do not usually occur immediately after a commitment to change, I have seen this man gradually change; he now smiles more, is more enthusiastic, and is more productive professionally. He is assertive in constructive ways; little of the old passivity is visible. Gone is his belief that magic will make things better. He continues to learn that *he* can make things better.

This tendency to believe in magic seems to gain more force in marriage, since marriage easily becomes the embodiment of magical expectations. But you can decide to start clearing the deck of magical expectations for marriage by making a conscious decision to change. You will be surprised at how quickly you pick up the new direction once you have made the commitment.

Realistic Expectations

As a belief in magic in marriage subsides, what can a person realistically expect? Realistic expectations might be called the Bill of Human Rights for Intimacy.

Although it is unrealistic to demand that marriage or intimacy bear the entire burden of meeting our needs, intimates do have the right to expect fair treatment. No intimate should settle for less than collaboration, an attitude of respect, honesty, and forgiveness.

Collaboration

Through research in business and industry, psychologists Robert Blake and Jane Mouton have effectively demonstrated that when obedience to authority figures is replaced by sharing of goals by employer and employee, people work together better and become more productive. Collaboration means that authority is distributed within and between levels of management and non-management. As the whole organization participates in decision-making, commitment to work toward shared goals deepens. According to research, collaborative leadership creates higher producing units, better morale, and lower turnover rates.

Imagine that same collaborative leadership style within the framework of intimacy. Instead of a typical pattern, where one person assumes more authority and the other assumes a passive role, genuine collaboration between equals takes place. When intimates collaborate and share authority, more is accomplished because neither feels forced. There is higher motivation and greater commitment to goals. If one person feels he must "obey," there will be only surface obedience and conformity. Underlying resentment and obstructive behavior will occur to block working together.

Collaboration in order to reach group goals also

achieves results in families, whether the problems are minor or major. The following example illustrates how this principle worked with a family in psychotherapy.

In the first therapy interview, an anxious mother gave the following brief history.

She had been divorced for two years, and the family was without a father figure. Her fourteen-year-old daughter had run away from home after being sent out of class for misbehavior—i.e., refusing to come to class on time, talking back to the teacher, and not studying. In addition, there was constant conflict at home between the daughter and her sixteen-year-old brother, who teased her continuously. A third child, a ten-year-old girl, was an average student but did as little as possible at home to help.

Since the whole family needed to work together, the family, not just the daughter, became the "patient." During the first family therapy session, the sixteen-year-old son stared at the floor with a sullen expression. The fourteen-year-old girl was hostile, yet appeared sensitive. The conversation began with an explanation that the family had a problem and needed to talk about it to solve it. Everyone in the family had a responsibility to help, since everyone had a stake in the solution.

There are no quick solutions to entrenched family problems such as this one, but a decision to work on specific areas starts the process of change. Because this family group finally decided to work together, everyone in it benefited by decisions regarding action to be taken. After three sessions, the son's face had changed noticeably; the grimness and pout were gone. He looked up and made eye contact. He was apparently more pleased with himself. His grades were going up through more effort on his part, and he was teasing his sister less. The runaway had returned to school and had received no bad conduct marks since the first family therapy session. Her attitude was more positive, and she appeared happier. The mother was relieved that, at least for the present, she was not being opposed as an authority figure. As the family observed specific changes, their motivation to continue these changes also increased.

Individual therapy with the runaway daughter, or with her mother, might have helped some, but not in time to alter family relationships. It is also highly doubtful that the older girl's misbehavior in the classroom would have decreased immediately with individual psychotherapy. Changing the authority system in the family to one of collaboration made the difference.

Only some of the more obvious symptoms of problems in this family were being dealt with, but the move toward collaboration created a healthier unit and made significant changes more likely. As a family system functions more effectively through collaboration, individual problems are more easily solved without the need of a psychotherapist.

Eventually, collaboration in intimacy means

- a regard for individual differences with equality between adults;
- an open discussion of important mattters, with agreements or compromises reached by discussion (not commands);
- clarification of group goals being worked toward together.

Custom plus sex-role training have created a situation where more authority often resides with the male intimate. This factor impedes collaboration with a resulting loss of morale, and with an ineffectual use of individual talent. Collaboration, which includes equal distribution of authority between male and female, is in the best interest of both sexes.

We have the right to expect collaboration from intimates. But we should expect more than that; we should expect respect, and refuse to settle for less.

Respect

Respect, another human right, is the cornerstone of caring. To be respected means to be treated as a human being of value, one with a separate identity. When we see our intimate as a person with a separate identity, his/her needs become as important as our own. Valuing our intimate's needs is the key here. Even if love and liking disappear, respect for an intimate as a person of worth can remain unchanged. Even if persons divorce, a mutual respect is possible.

The practice of respect for an intimate may be blocked in several ways. Distractions, preoccupations, and unexpressed negative feelings often communicate to an intimate a lack of respect. A common weekend message, for example, is "Televised football is more important than talking to you." Such behavior does speak louder than words to the contrary.

Attention to what our mate says is one measure of our respect. Too often we hear the words of a conversation but do not really hear the message. Listening to words and hearing the message are quite different. A response such as "Yes, dear, you had a hard day," after a spouse talks about problems at the office is not the same as "You are really wrestling with some knotty problems with your colleagues. Let me see if I understand what is going on." The involvement, interest, and effort to help are unmistakable in the latter statement, which shows hearing, while the former comment is an example of perfunctory listening to words and responding with a descriptive cliche.

Respect practiced daily prevents damage to an intimate when problems exist, and provides a climate where problems are more likely to be solved.

Ineffectual communication may contribute to our intimate's experiencing a low level of respect in marriage. We may feel love and respect deeply, yet be unable to communicate those feelings in a way that is meaningful to our intimates. Yet where do we receive any training in how to show respect for others? To *feel* love and respect for an intimate is not enough; our intimate needs to *experience* those feelings. Therefore, in order to communicate respect, we need to be aware of how our intimate perceives respect so that we can match our actions and words with his/her understanding.

The best way to determine how an intimate perceives respect, or the absence of it, is to ask. There are few problems that cannot be solved by open discussion of attitudes and actions and what they convey. We can speed change by pointing out where respect is communicated. Intimates need to know when they are on the right track, not just when they're on the wrong one, and a positive approach is usually more helpful than a negative one.

Unexpressed negative feelings can interfere with the ability to be aware of a mate's needs. However, there is *never* an excuse to damage an intimate's self-esteem. We can express anger or a variety of negative feelings without harming a relationship, if we practice respect.

One wife in group therapy explained how learning to express negative feelings had helped her resolve resentments and become more aware of her husband's needs. For years she had resented her husband's working in their home late at night. Through the years, she had subtly nagged him to leave his work at the office.

As a result of group therapy training, she began to express directly to her husband both a desire to be with him and a feeling of neglect when he shut her out. Once she expressed her resentment openly, she was able to get past her own feelings so that she could listen to his. She began to see the financial pressure he experienced, the demands of his job, and his commitment to doing his work well. Negative feelings had kept her from being objective about her intimate's needs.

One evening when he was working late on a tax report, she stayed up to read a book. From the next room she could hear him shuffling papers and swearing softly. Acknowledging his need for understanding, she went to him and said, "I know how tiring it is filling out those forms. Would you like a drink?"

"I'll get a drink in a minute!" he snapped, but she noticed as she went back to her book that he became less restless. Half an hour later he emerged in a good mood with the work completed.

By sensing his need for appreciation, this woman showed awareness of the situation and consideration for her intimate's feelings. Her action demonstrated genuine respect and helped him complete his work with patience.

Honesty

Another right in intimacy is honesty.

The honesty that counts most is a state of being honest about feelings, reactions, and attitudes. All of us are prone to self-deception, and sometimes need help to be aware of our feelings. We can, however, be as honest as possible with an intimate. Honesty that helps intimacy does not violate an intimate's rights as a separate person. The misuse of honesty cripples the vitality of an intimate, and prevents personal growth.

Respect for a mate's right to separateness, and trust in mutual commitment, does not imply that to be honest one must tell all the details of one's life and one's thoughts. The idea of total honesty in any relationship is unrealistic. Real honesty is honesty in being, not in telling. After all, it is possible to disclose all the details of one's life and still not disclose oneself.

People intuitively understand their own need for privacy, but they are often unable to allow it in someone they love.

To expect your mate to tell you every thought and deed is to treat an adult as a child. Even children, as they develop a sense of identity and individuality, are not expected to tell their parents everything.

Telling all the details of one's life is "content honesty." In contrast, honesty in being involves revealing how you are as a person at a given time. A sharing of attitudes and feelings reveals more about you as a person than does a description of events. Comments which add up to "This is where I stand" or "This is who I am" are a personal revelation while "I had lunch with John today" may or may not tell anything about the person speaking.

For example, the husband of one patient appears to be a model mate and father. He tells his wife what happens to him at work each day and helps discipline the children at night. He helps balance his wife's checking account and smoothes over any ruffled feelings she may have collected during the day. Although he shares some of the details of his life at a descriptive level, he shares little of himself. Heavily protected behind the masks of the roles he plays, he reveals few personal reactions. His conversation is superficial, and he does not share his own thinking. He relates on the surface, so that his innermost feelings and attitudes are seldom revealed. His wife experiences guilt feelings because she is unhappy with him and cannot understand why, since he does most of the things expected of a mate.

This couple is suffering from an impoverished emotional relationship. The husband has learned that to avoid being hurt one does not show feelings, take a position on anything, or admit problems. He is dishonest in his pattern of living, since he does not reveal himself. As long as he relates like a mannikin, he risks showing only his facade—a very "safe" transaction for him. His wife experiences intimacy frustration because she wants and needs more from him in the relationship. Actually she is not yet aware that he is not being honest as a person.

The husband can begin to change; motivation to be himself may begin with a realization that his wife needs more from him now. Being himself, which is the essence of honesty, is necessary for their intimacy satisfaction. Even with motivation to change, some time is needed to lay aside the armor of facade.

A psychotherapist may help you change more easily,

but you can start by expressing personal feelings and ideas as they occur to you—with your intimate, and with selected friends at work. I can assure you that the personal satisfaction you will experience is worth any temporary discomfort which accompanies change.

We often learn as children that the expression of personal feelings is dangerous. As we progress in our ability to be emotionally honest, some discomfort serves as a reminder of that lesson, until we experience the rewards of better intimacy from being open.

Being oneself—being authentic—creates an atmosphere of trust, where a mate is more likely to be real in response to your authenticity. Being oneself means communicating real feelings and thoughts so that an intimate does not have to guess at what is happening in the relationship. This is the essence of honesty as a state of being. This kind of honesty is realistic for intimates to expect.

Forgiveness

Another human right in intimacy is the right to expect forgiveness from an intimate. Because of the inevitable hurt feelings in an intimacy, forgiveness is a necessary part of a relationship. Forgiveness means pardoning someone for injury you experienced from him/her in a relationship.

The process of building forgiveness into intimacy requires an honest expression of hurt feelings; an openness to receive this information; a response to "repair" the damage to an intimate; and an act of forgiveness toward the intimate who offended.

The psychological dynamics of the process of forgiveness are illustrated by the following incident.

A husband and wife gave a company party and invited secretaries, business associates, and a few out-of-town guests. This man spent literally the whole evening with one secretary and two associates, with the result that his wife felt left out and unimportant. (Her feeling of unimportance was a direct response to her husband's involvement with others and his lack of involvement with her.)

This couple had learned the value of open communication in group therapy. Instead of criticizing her husband for ignoring her, or accusing him of being flirtatious, the wife was able to explain to him afterward that she had felt left out and replaced by others at the party. The direct expression of feelings helped to reduce her sense of injury as a result of being left out.

Whether she was justified in feeling injured is not the issue. A common pitfall with intimates is to argue about concrete happenings instead of dealing with personal feelings. When feelings are dealt with, concrete problems will be resolved.

Her husband perceived that she felt hurt and he was sorry. He did not need to justify his behavior or to engage in discussion about who was right. The important facts were feelings.

By being responsible for her feelings, she paved the way for him to respond non-defensively. Instead of making accusations or calling names, she reported how *she* felt.

By dealing with her problem openly and directly she stimulated her husband to respond in a way that actually built up her self-esteem without damaging his. He felt genuinely sorry for having contributed to her hurt, and she was able to forgive without holding a grudge. No actual damage was done to the relationship, and a large hurdle to intimacy was successfully overcome.

Remember that your act of pardoning your intimate has a double benefit to you: You will let go of grudges and develop a forgiving attitude toward others—a decided asset to your happiness and that of your intimate!

In place of the idea that "marriage will make you happy," we have certain realistic rights, a Bill of Human Rights, that we should expect in intimacy and marriage. Once the importance of these is established, we are in a bettter position to consider the issue of children.

"Children Will Make Me Happy"

In the midst of disillusionment about magic in marriage, some couples may reason that if something dramatically new were attempted, the Promised Land of marital bliss would be discovered. Since children are considered to be a natural outgrowth of marriage, it is not surprising that mates often see having a child as a new hope for personal and marital happiness. A favorite subfiction to "marriage will make me happy," then, is the notion that "children will make me happy."

Sociologists generally agree that the family is the central group which gives us the feeling of belonging. As a couple expands to include children, a heightened sense of belonging develops. Despite this feeling of belonging, however, and the social status which accompanies parenthood, couples may also lose considerable independence. Knowing which values have priority for you is important in determining whether you really want children. Let's put aside magic for a moment and consider the pros and cons of children's effects on intimacy.

Children: An asset

On the positive side, children are an expression of a couple's creative activity. As a marriage expands to become a group in which other persons live and develop, isolation shrinks. Too, a couple may acquire a new sense of shared purpose with the advent of children.

A child can catalyze dormant areas of a parent's personality, stimulating adult growth. A child by his/her example may teach a parent that it is all right to be independent. The child may arouse in a parent the wish to give, thereby reassuring even the cynical that, deep within us, there is a need to give to other human beings.

In addition to stimulating the parents' ability to give, the child frequently enlarges the parents' social awareness by involving them more fully in community life through school and social activities.

Similarly, identity with a family group offers a secure base of caring and concern in the midst of the growing anonymity of life in metropolitan areas.

Finally, children offer a sense of continuity to a family group that extends beyond the parents' own lifetimes.

Children: A liability

On the negative side, two people in love often find their own world shattered by cries in the night, dirty diapers, and general confinement to the home. Privacy is largely eliminated by young children. A "turned on" sex life, which demands spontaneity and time, may be dimmed by knocks on the closed door or by the usual noises that children make.

Children in our modern society are expensive, and the cost of food, clothing, education, and medical care goes up yearly. The fact that money problems often contribute heavily to marital discord means that children may prove to be the straw that breaks the back of a marriage.

Some couples have all the problems they can cope with, without children. A child may add to an already heavy burden of responsibility in a marriage, or block a woman from a promising career. Worse, a child may be the reason two people stay in a relationship they would otherwise terminate.

In summary, there is no evidence that children, by some magic, make intimacy better.

Are You Ready for Children?

After considering the pros and cons of child-rearing, some intimates may decide that they are ready for children. Other couples may decide that it is better not to have children. Some men and women are not child-oriented; the world of children bores them, makes demands on their time, and intrudes excessively on their private lives. While most parents have such feelings some of the time, some women and men have them most of the time. There is nothing necessarily the matter with people who honestly do not wish to have children of their own. Acknowledging this fact is important in preventing a premature decision to have children.

Some women like children but do not want to give birth to their own. Susan has a happy marriage, and a job as a welfare worker for dependent and neglected children. She gives herself fully to the job of protecting the welfare of children and advising parents in child guidance. When she comes home, she enjoys quiet intimacy with her spouse, and a mutual give-and-take. Her day is filled with giving to children, but she does not want more of it at night. Her husband, her co-workers, and a caseload of children meet Susan's needs for intimacy, a sense of achievement, and belonging. She is honest enough to admit that she does not want children now, and courageous enough to withstand social pressures from relatives.

What about that individual who discovers *after* childbirth that rearing children is not his/her cup of tea? Such a parent may choose either to be as much of a parent as possible or to turn most of the child-rearing over to the mate (if he/she is willing). If neither parent wishes to bear the brunt of parental responsibility, the couple may hire a maid so that someone will cope with the child's daily routine and supply the needed nurturing. Sometimes a person other than a parent is more capable of meeting the child's emotional needs. What matters is the quality of time spent with a child. Besides, the more adults involved with the child-rearing the better, since mistakes are better compensated for in this way, and more adults are available as models.

Yet, even if a couple wants children, they may not necessarily be ready to rear them well. Most parents want to rear children effectively, but find a book by Spock or Ginott is not enough to prepare them adequately. Classes for parents in basic principles of child-rearing should be available, or even required by law, before the birth of the first child.

To compensate more completely for the fact that parents are usually not trained educators or experts in human behavior, we need facilities for early childhood education. A model child development center for children under five would provide expert training for children of the affluent and poor alike. According to our current knowledge, a well-developed personality structure during these formative years would prevent most serious mental illnesses, break the poverty cycle, and accelerate each child's emotional and academic development.

Not only is it desirable that parents really want children and know something about child-rearing, but also that they have an intimacy that includes most of the realistic expectations discussed in this chapter.

* * *

The fiction that marriage, or children, will make one happy causes disillusionment that robs many an intimacy of life. Somehow we have been brainwashed to believe that, by some magic, our needs will be met in marriage and our purposes in life fulfilled. Such a notion is unrealistic. On the other hand, if genuine collaboration takes place, and our actions toward each other demonstrate respect, honesty, and forgiveness, we will be happier in intimacy. We can progress out of magical expectations toward the fundamentals of intimacy, and we should not expect less of ourselves or of our intimates than a demonstrated effort in that direction.

7 | The Meaning of Sex in Our Lives

When you hear the word "sex," what comes to mind? Bed? Body? Pleasure? The meaning would be a personal one; for when it comes to sex, we live by the meaning it has for us.

Knowledge has dispelled many fictions about sex, adding to our peace of mind. We know that:

- Children have sexual feelings, though they are not the same as adults'.
- Persons over seventy-five may have an active sex life.
- Sexual feelings toward the same sex do not mean homosexuality, and are quite common.
- Sexual frigidity or impotence is learned behavior.
- Most sexual problems can be solved by education, training, or psychotherapy.
- Sexual acts are physical *and* psychological.
- Sexual fantasies are common in adults.
- It is natural to want sex with more than one person of the opposite sex.

Even in the face of scientific knowledge, fictions about sex disappear slowly. Regardless of the current openness about sex, we still tend to think of it primarily in terms of an act or a drive somehow fragmented from the total person. And there is still much confusion that exists concerning

- sexual identity—
- sexual roles—
- sexuality—
- sexual actions.

Let's look at some definitions in order to get a clearer perspective of the meaning of sex in our lives.

Sexual Identity

A sexual fiction emerging today is the notion that we are not born with a sexual identity as males and females, but that we learn to be male and female only by sex-role training. This idea that all sex differences are environmentally produced is a notion which has been thoroughly discredited by psychological research on sex differences and similarities. But this new illusion has grown to the point where sexual equality is confused with sexual sameness. A deeper understanding of sexual identity that includes more than physical features and stereotyped sex roles is needed to cut through fictions. Let me illustrate my point with an unusual example which demonstrates that sexual identity is primarily a state of awareness of one's membership in one sex or the other. At birth the brain signals whether one is male or female, and this is the basis for awareness of one's sex identity.

The transsexual is a person with a basic psychological identity (male or female) who, by a freak of nature, is born with a body, including genitals, of the opposite sex. This physical identification with the opposite sex, present from birth, does not change with puberty. With a high hormone count of the other sex and few secondary sex characteristics, the transsexual believes he or she is trapped in the wrong body. This is not true of the homosexual, who likes his/her body. Neither is it true of the transvestite, who wears clothing of the opposite sex, nor of the person who has psychotic delusions that he/she is of the opposite sex.

A definition of sexual identity as a function of cultural training or physical characteristics is not adequate. Social training to be male or female doubtless has its effects, but training to act male or female does not create the nuclear identity of a male or female person. The transsexual teaches us that sexual identity is not merely the result of environmental conditioning, or the presence of genital organs of a certain sex, but is essentially psychological.

In other words, sexual identity is primarily *psychological awareness* of being one or the other sex.

Sexual Roles

Some people convey the attitude that males and females have certain fixed characteristics and should express their identity through roles defined by social custom. Training for these roles begins early in life, when boys are taught to play with guns and girls with dolls. It carries over into adulthood; men are expected to hunt and fish, or "earn the bread," and women are expected to keep house. Those whose interests lie outside of areas normally sanctioned by society as appropriate may experience rejection. In spite of increasingly enlightened attitudes, eyebrows are still raised if a man says, "I cook, clean the house, and take care of the children while my wife works."

Sexuality and Sexual Actions

Sexuality is the total expression of one's state of being as male or female, and may be emphasized or deemphasized by body posture, dress, mannerisms, words, and touch. Although intangible at times, sexuality is usually unmistakable. It is reflected in the attitude which says, "I am glad to be a sexual creature," a message quite different from a painted on, plastic sex appeal. Sexuality involves being a person, one who is at home with his or her sexual feelings and characteristics.

One can communicate intense sexuality *(being)* without overt sexual activity *(doing)*. Sexual actions are what we do with our sexuality and may involve a very low or a high degree of sexuality. Lovemaking with much sexuality is usually a warm, intense, caring, and involved experience. Lovemaking without much sexuality may be physically satisfying but emotionally barren and impersonal. Sex without sexuality leaves one with an empty feeling.

Some of the distinctions between sexual identity, sexual roles, sexuality, and sexual actions may be demonstrated by a look at the case of Sue, who was seen in psychotherapy.

An attractive airline stewardess, Sue had a negative relationship with her mother, who criticized her continually and undermined her confidence. Sue's mother was unhappy about herself and taught Sue through her actions that being a woman was boring, depressing, and frustrating. As a result, Sue was not at ease with her sexual identity, since she was unsure whether she really wanted to be a woman.

As a result, lacking self-confidence, she played at being a woman by being what men wanted her to be without the risk of emotional involvement. Because of her good looks, it was easy for Sue to find males who would collaborate with her pattern of achieving approval from them by responding sexually. Yet while she could relate sexually to men, she did so mainly at a superficial level which gave her a safety zone.

As Sue began to explore her feelings about herself in psychotherapy, and to like and trust herself more, she began to discover who she was as a female person and to accept her sexual identity. Instead of playing at being a woman, she began to show more of her inner self. Sue actually felt more feminine as she grew more assertive and expressive. By being true to her thoughts and feelings, she was truer to herself as a woman. She became less concerned with society's expectations, refusing to be boxed in by stereotyped sex roles. If she wanted to meet a male, she gave herself the freedom to deal herself into the relationship. Males who insisted on playing certain roles became threatened because she would not play games, while others welcomed Sue's freedom to be herself as a benefit to both. Her unique personality became more noticeable.

As Sue progressed in psychotherapy, she moved from being superficially sexy to being sexual, and people reacted instantly to the sexuality she communicated. Because sexuality is a manifestation of one's sexual identity, Sue became more herself as her sexuality was expressed. Instead of preening before a mirror for two hours before a date, she began to use less makeup. She remained well-groomed and striking in appearance without an artificial quality of being "too perfect." Men found her more attractive and felt drawn to her as a person who owned and felt at home with her sexual feelings. Women also related to her. As she began to accept herself, she was able to accept other women as individuals and as friends without seeing them as competitors.

In accepting her sexuality, she became a complete person.

Sexual Freedom

Before psychotherapy helped Sue develop a sense of who she was, she was often confused about how to express herself sexually. If she admitted sexual feelings, she either became afraid of losing control, or impulsively expressed the feelings by sexual acts ranging from petting to intercourse. She was often confused about the appropriate sexual action, as if she needed to write a script for herself to follow.

As Sue learns to understand herself better, her sense of personhood and self-trust will be strengthened. She now bases her decisions about sexual expression on a combination of her feelings about who she *is,* who she *wants* to be, and how she authentically reacts to a *specific* male.

By integrating sexual thoughts with sexual feelings, she moves toward reconciling the typical mind/feeling dichotomy and has more control over her actions. For example, she may feel like making love to a man she has known for only a short period of time, or she may choose to postpone action until she feels she knows him better. Her decision is determined by what the relationship means to her. By allowing her feelings to be transparent, she is also honest in the relationship. In this manner, she has genuine freedom to be the person she actually is.

Before, Sue had never achieved freedom to choose, since she had decided on sexual actions according to apparent social norms and had acted compulsively on her sexual feelings. She is now making conscious choices, based on who she is and who she wants to be as a person. Only in this context will sex have more personal meaning for her. And persons live by meaning, not sensation, with sex.

The Meanings of Sex

My theoretical position is that sex has many levels of meaning, but that meaning is primarily a function of a unique encounter between two persons. Sex can be misused in many ways. It can be

- exploitative,
- commercialized,

- dehumanized,
- a camouflage for problems.

On the positive side, sex can be

- fun,
- communication,
- ecstasy,
- commitment,
- self-regard,
- sensitivity,
- dependency,
- intimacy.

Let's look more closely at some of these meanings, both negative and positive.

Sex Exploited

When males or females use sex to control, sex becomes a tool for exploitation.

One basic, widespread fiction places men and women in the role of mutual exploiters: the notion that woman's primary value consists of the sexual favors she can offer. Even sophisticated adults fall prey to this notion. According to the fiction, once a woman has bestowed her favors, she is no longer of value. The idea that man's sexual expression *per se* has no value, and woman's sexual expression nullifies her value, is highly destructive to intimacy.

A corollary to the fiction that woman's primary value is what she can give sexually is the concept that man is out to rob her of this value. This notion sets the stage for sexual exploitation.

First, assumedly, the male is out to exploit the female, so for protection the female must exploit the male in return. Sex becomes part of a transaction that denies a person's value. The fiction further suggests that in order for a woman not to be devalued by sex she should acquire something in return. Although fiction is somewhat vague at this point, the implication is that marriage and/or security are worthwhile values in return.

In reality, sexual expression has value as the expression of a person, and males and females have equal value as persons. Moreover, the value of the person is not exhausted by the expression. So how can exploitation take place when each shares the value in sexual expression?

Sex Commercialized

Doubtless you've noticed that every time you open a magazine or turn on the television set, sex is used to sell you some product. Slinky creatures atop shiny automobiles try to convince you that their company has the best offer. This hair tonic or that cologne will ensure your sexual desirability, and even toothpaste promises to provide you with sex appeal.

With the deluge of sex as a marketable item, it is no wonder we have over-glamorized it. No wonder a couple suspects that something is wrong, either with themselves or with their marriage, when they do not experience immediate and sustained sexual ecstasy.

If sex is seen as a commodity that one must "put on" or purchase, it becomes something apart from persons. But sex is basically part of one's personality and sexual expression an aspect of oneself. One does not become more sexual by the purchase of anything. Even books on sex tend to dehumanize. Books and manuals on how to perform better sexually may provide interesting instructions about sex techniques at a mechanical level, but may overlook basic attitudes that cause problems in the first place.

Yes, sex will help sell books, cars, and a wide assortment of products. The truth is, however, that sex draws us to persons, not objects, and is a way of communicating person to person. To the extent that we treat each other as persons, we are being more sexual. To the extent that we treat other as objects, we contribute to "sex commercialized."

Sex Dehumanized

Equally destructive is the tendency to view sex as something sacred in order not to see it as "evil." Such thinking leads to inhibitions destructive to relationships and fragments sex from the rest of life.

Archaic attitudes which see sex as bad—something to be inhibited or tolerated rather than enjoyed—are currently on the mend. But the idea that enjoying a sexual relationship is somehow "wicked" still remains in many minds, and a marriage ceremony alone does not erase this idea.

Any attitude which communicates that sex is not essentially good is life-negating. Positive attitudes toward sex, and fully functioning sexual relationships, are important to personality well-being.

When a marriage ceremony is required to "purify" sex, a subtle form of dehumanization takes place. Sex is elevated out of the realm of the human and provided with a magical aura, as if to justify its existence.

In spite of increasing premarital sexual freedom, many unconsciously believe that sexual feelings and actions are not desirable unless sanctioned by society. Negative sex attitudes are often transferred to the marriage relationship where people do not feel any better about sex after marriage than before.

Sex as part of human existence needs no justification. When the individual accepts his right to decide about his or her sexual expression, he takes sex out of the realm of impersonal rules, codes, and social custom and puts it back where it belongs—within the realm of personal choice.

Sex as a Camouflage for Problems

Unfortunately, sex is commonly misused to avoid facing problems.

Take Sarah and Jim. Jim's solution to every argument is to end tension by having sex with his wife. However, it takes Sarah longer to cool off and sort out her emotions before she can respond sexually. If she gratifies her husband before she is emotionally and physically ready, she will not relax or experience much sensual satisfaction. She experiences increased resentment instead.

Actually Jim's solution tends to reinforce arguments if he sees sex as a "reward" at the end. But using sex to end an argument may prevent them from seeing an argument through to a workable solution, or at least to a compromise.

If Sarah can be honest with Jim, she might say, "I am tense now; I don't feel like lovemaking," or "I would like to respond to you, but I am not ready now to open up." Authentic communication may discourage his use of sex to ease tensions following disagreements.

Satisfying sex does reduce tensions, but sex without emotional preparation leaves Sarah more tense with a feeling of being misunderstood. In this context sex becomes, without her husband's awareness, a tool to cover up problems. If mates see what is behind a "sexual problem," sex can function in the service of uncovering problems in intimacy.

*   *   *

Sex can be used in the service of many positive experiences. The positive meanings of sex seem to greatly outnumber the negative ones. Let's look at some of the ways sex can be a fulfilling experience with positive meanings.

Sex Is Fun

One positive approach to sex is as "fun and games." Outside of marriage this attitude might be labeled "playing," and sex would be defined as something to be enjoyed between two people without obligation, responsibility, or commitment.

But why limit fun to relationships outside of marriage? Sex in marriage or intimacy is not always a serious business.

Sex as fun implies sex for the sheer enjoyment of it, and delight in the experience. No sense of coercion is present when two people are spontaneously having a good time.

A playful attitude, at least during the preliminary stages of the sex act, enhances the total enjoyment that takes places between a man and woman. If one can regress in an appropriate manner, being childlike and provocative, emotional intensity is built up. Besides, there is evidence that when fun and playfulness are left out of a relationship, sexual desire decreases.

Ralph, for example, had trouble having any fun at all. He told me in therapy, "I work hard and play hard." Actually he did not play at all. Overly serious and driven to be a success, he lost his capacity to play. His "child," or the playful part of his personality, was crushed under a burden of work. Ultimately he had trouble turning off his intellect so that he could feel his own body sensations and could enjoy touching his mate.

Analysis of the basis of his "overdrive" and a decision to change opened up space to play. Gradually, he learned to fondle, caress, and kiss his wife for increasingly long periods of time before actual intercourse.

Since he allowed himself plenty of time for the preliminaries, he was able to make intercourse last longer, which in turn maximized his wife's pleasure. Prolonged play before intercourse aroused her more, and a longer time together made heightened responses possible. His enjoyment in giving her pleasure increased his own. His change in approach was sufficiently rewarded to help produce a change in attitude toward play. "Sex play" began to mean just that to him.

Sex Is Communication

Experience in individual and group psychotherapy indicates that most communication is nonverbal or wordless in nature. Sex is an experience where husband and wife can communicate to each other a full range of emotional reactions. Through sex one can tell an intimate how much one really cares and how deeply one wishes to give.

I am reminded of a patient who is scientifically oriented, immersed in research, and preoccupied with theories. His wife says that he never tells her he loves her. Yet, during lovemaking she realizes that he tells her with his body what he cannot tell her with his vocal cords. Sex for him is an experience that transcends verbal communication and engages all his flexibility, sensitivity, and creativity.

Sex, essentially, is one way to communicate. So sex problems are really communication problems.

One patient, Mr. W., found himself making excuses for not having intercourse with his wife. He was not aware of underlying resentments which blocked feelings of warmth and affection. He resented the fact that she had become busy in club organizations and was not always waiting for him when he arrived home. Instead of discussing this with her, he allowed his feelings of indignation to form a wall that blocked the communication of affection.

Once he was able to face the reasons for his resentments and resolve them through open discussion with his wife, his sexual interests were revived, and serious problems in the marriage were avoided.

Sex Is Ecstasy

Enjoying sex involves a factor often ignored: the ability to surrender self-control. The fact that so many people fall short of their sexual potential is due to this aspect of the sexual relationship.

Part of the problem is our almost primeval fear of being overpowered by forces beyond our control. The ability to relax control is essential to increased sexual enjoyment.

The paradox of control in the sexual relationship is the need for a sensitive awareness of the time required to satisfy one's mate, and the ability to release one's inhibitions. A relaxed attitude and a gradual build-up of sensations, combined with expression of tender yet passionate feelings, leads to optimum enjoyment in the relationship. If emotional brakes are applied by either person and there is anxiety about the loss of control, ecstasy is missed.

Genuine control over one's emotions allows one the freedom to lose control as a function of choice. Passion can be so ecstatic as to render conscious thought impossible and to allow complete submergence of the self in gratifying both body and mind. In such a state, and between persons who care, passion may be uncontrolled, but not out of control. By willing ourselves to be open and receptive to ecstasy, we are in control of our own joy.

Sex Is Dependency

A common problem that blocks sustained sexual openness is fear of dependency. Forgotten feelings of helplessness can be aroused in intimacy, reminding us that we are dependent on another, thus creating anxiety.

One case illustrates how this fear operates.

One night after sexual foreplay, a young husband-of-one-year became impotent directly before penetration for intercourse. Much anxiety followed, motivating him to start psychotherapy. He understood, after short-term therapy, that his relationship with his wife had deepened to a point where he was afraid to become closer. He had learned from his mother that it was "dangerous to be dependent." Being more intimate meant being more dependent, a thought which caused him considerable anxiety.

By concentration one can cut off sensation, in a kind of self-hypnosis, almost anywhere in the body. Through fear, the patient had literally "cut off" feelings in his penis with a resulting inability to maintain erection for intercourse.

While he was under hypnosis, the suggestion was made that he reject the taboo against dependency. In giving this message to his body, he could again begin to feel sensations in the genital area.

In a relatively short time the patient became completely potent again. He reached a new height of sexual intensity with his wife and experienced deeper feelings than before. When fear returned and he would start to lose an erection, he would relax, understanding what was happening, and the fear would subside without a loss of erection.

His fear of dependency was not completely resolved, but its effect on his sexual enjoyment was dissipated.

Sex Is Sensitivity

What does sensitivity to feelings have to do with sex?

In my opinion, too much stress has been placed on sexual technique and not enough on sexual sensitivity. No amount of technical training in the biological functions of sex, nor the mastery of countless sexual positions, can take the place of awareness of the emotional life of one's intimate. This includes a sensitive awareness of emotional changes in the other person. Whether a person is angry, disappointed, or tense is important, since emotions are so intricately tied to the act of sex.

Timing is an important part of sensitivity. Take the case of a husband who has had a hard day at the office. Unless he has had an opportunity to relax from the day's problems, amorous feelings do not arise. Or take the case of a wife who has been bearing the responsibility of two small children during the day. Is she likely to feel "turned on" sexually before the children are asleep?

In each of the cases above, sensitivity to feelings and timing is essential to create an atmosphere where sexual feelings are aroused.

Sex Is Intimacy

The more common problem in our culture is not the avoidance of sex, but the avoidance of intimacy. And intimacy is necessary to keep the sparks of sexual desire alive over a period of time.

To open up to sexual expression in the context of deep feelings of love, it is necessary to tolerate being vulnerable. Tolerance of vulnerability is only possible if there is trust in the relationship. To bare oneself in the act of love requires the utmost trust, confidence, and risk-taking.

Intimacy problems are actually common to all of us. My personal experience as a patient in group therapy was more than part of my training; it was a vital step in self-development. The following dream illustrates my personal battle to conquer fear of intimacy and learned social taboos against getting close.

In the dream I found myself leaving an auditorium naked after a concert. I experienced the feeling that it was all right to be naked, but felt mild embarrassment at not being dressed appropriately. Hoping people would not notice, I headed for the parking lot. On the way to the car, I thought, "I might get arrested for indecent exposure."

My fiancée was waiting in the car. As I glanced to the left, I saw a policeman standing a short distance away. He said, "The best place for someone like you is in a mental hospital. You're crazy!"

The act of leaving the auditorium represented a movement away from social norms. I felt a sense of being a separate person, apart from the crowd. Although I was aware of my body as good, I also sensed social disapproval. In the parking lot, I experienced the taboo of feeling guilty for breaking rules, and faced an expectation of punishment.

The fiancée waiting in the car symbolized an openness to intimacy and closeness. But in the car I faced the injunction that it is "crazy" to be intimate and close. The policeman symbolized an impersonal rule, very common in our achievement-oriented society: "Be heavily protected against intimacy, or face punishment, guilt, and insanity."

One of the dangers of such rules is that they operate as self-fulfilling prophecies. If a person does allow himself to be open to intimacy, he does so only tentatively, and will find evidence that his fear was well-grounded. He thus fulfills his own prophecy, proving to himself that it is dangerous to be intimate.

If we are going to change, we need to be in touch with the part of us that resists change. The following dialogue is an example of working through taboos against intimacy. The person *becomes* the positive wish to be intimate, conversing with the part of him that resists intimacy. Then he becomes the negative side and speaks to the positive aspect of himself, as follows:

POSITIVE: I want to be open and intimate with my mate. I am willing to take the chance of being hurt.

NEGATIVE: You're crazy to take a chance on getting close. You've been taught not to take risks. You've been protected for years this way.

POSITIVE: But protection isn't worth the price of losing the satisfaction possible with intimacy.

NEGATIVE: That's what you think. This is your final warning. Do not get close and open up.

POSITIVE: I have decided to be open sexually and emotionally.

NEGATIVE: Then you will be punished with guilt and anxiety.

POSITIVE: Shut up. I don't need your punishment anymore for control. My decision is final, and I like the rewards.

NEGATIVE: OK, but don't say I didn't warn you. And I haven't given up yet.

This kind of dialogue will be very real to the person, and feelings will be strong on both sides. Change may be slow to show, but increased intimacy without anxiety can result.

By experiencing both negative and positive sides of intimacy, some reconciliation of differences occurs. Being in touch with both aspects of one's personality helps provide control. Taking a stand against the negative side starts a process of change which will halt guilt and anxiety, and will pave the way for the positive side to dominate.

Sex Is Commitment

Sex as intimacy is related to sex as commitment. Sometimes sex is the only way two people can express their commitment—the revelation of each person's profound wish to be involved in the life of the other—in a way that is totally fulfilling at that moment. Commitment includes intimacy, and when sex is viewed as a part of the relationship between two people, it is a confirmation of their love for one another. Sex as a commitment or bond between two persons, whether they are married or not, can be a deeply fulfilling experience.

Words of Advice

To increase sexual happiness with your mate, work on the following suggestions:

- Do not be afraid to ask for sex. Even if you are turned down sometimes, ask again. (Nice girls can speak up about their wants!)
- Encourage your mate to ask for sex when in the mood.
- Show appreciation for your mate as a person before sex play begins. Be specific.
- Engage your mate's mind. Talk about your tender, passionate feelings.
- Really examine your mate's body, and talk openly about your feelings. "Get out of your head and come to your senses."
- Give more time for foreplay. Don't rush; find out more sensitive areas of the body. Repeat to men: More time for foreplay!
- Do tell the other person what you need to be sexually satisfied. Tell gently.
- Do not be afraid to let your inner child out and have fun. Be playful.
- Do not confine your amorous moments to sexual intercourse. Caress for its own sake.
- Keep romance in the marriage. Remember special dates, surprises, gifts, etc.
- Do not be afraid to risk being interdependent and intimate. The rewards are worth it.

And remember the cardinal rule: Take time to enjoy sex with your intimate.

* * *

If you have the feeling that marriage is a great sex swindle instead of a way of living happily sexually, you may want to rethink your understanding of sex. When you can see sex as *a part of,* rather than *apart from,* the totality of your life as man or woman, you will begin to understand and appreciate sex in all its meanings. And, when it comes to sex, we live more by meaning than sensation.

8 | *Autonomy Plus Collaboration Equals Enriched Intimacy*

The fiction "you belong to me" says that one intimate is the possession of another. Psychotherapy interviews with well over a thousand adults have convinced me that the attitude inherent in the fiction must change if intimacy is to be enjoyed for any period of time. Yet this attitude is so commonplace that we can all identify with it.

In an intimacy where we really care—in or out of marriage—the monster of possessiveness often creeps in to strangle caring. Is possessiveness a natural tendency, or did we learn it?

At the bottom of possessiveness is the positive desire to stay in a meaningful relationship. What is innate, then, is a desire to be part of a two-person group (or larger one) and solve the problem of aloneness. Attempts to keep a relationship intact can be easily diverted into possessive channels, so that what is natural becomes expressed in an unnatural way. "You belong to me" is so commonplace in intimacy that it seems natural on the surface. Hence the deceptive phrase: "It is natural to be possessive."

The desire to possess is created out of our own insecurities. That is, as we find our personal needs being met in an intimacy, we wish to make the relationship a secure one. In misguided attempts to protect the relationship, we create the fiction that "you belong to me" and build a prison for intimates.

Especially in marriage does the "you belong to me" myth run rampant. Husbands and wives often view each other as possessions, transforming persons into objects and dehumanizing intimacy.

The person being possessed is as guilty as the possessor if he/she relinquishes self-identity for fear of losing a valued relationship. Possessiveness does not make a relationship more secure, but less secure, and kills opportunities for personal growth in intimacy. "You belong to me" practiced means, ultimately, the end of aliveness and joy in an intimacy. The apparent security of "you belong to me" is a cruel deception, yet humans are fully capable of eliminating possessiveness.

The realization that one belongs first to oneself and that one's mate has the same right to autonomy is a powerful antidote to the desire to possess or be possessed. In fact, such a realization is essential to an alive marriage and a growing intimacy. When one mate does not respect—much less support—the developing autonomy of the other, a destructive process is at work in the relationship and intimacy is ultimately injured. Intimacy is enjoyable only as long as the two intimates respect each other's right to belong to themselves.

The rest of this chapter is devoted to ways of identifying the illusion that "you belong to me" and suggestions on how to defeat it. The key word in changing illusion to reality is *separate*.

Separate Interests

One way partners attempt to possess is by belittling a mate's separate interests. One husband criticizes his wife's paintings, calling them unrealistic and amateur. He says that her hobby, which in reality serves as an important outlet for her creativity and emotional energy, keeps her from having time to be an adequate housewife. His complaint is that it "costs too much money, takes up too much room, and is too messy."

A wife mutters about her husband's golf, to which he devotes nearly every Sunday afternoon. He should, in her opinion, be mowing the lawn or fixing the shutters. She ignores the fact that he puts in a fifty-hour work week that makes extensive emotional demands on him.

Another way partners attempt to possess is by demanding that an intimate make a choice between interests, or work, and family. Mary insists that her husband spend more time at home and less at the office, a demand which impales him on the horns of a dilemma of guilt. If he spends less time at the office and more time at home to please her, he feels guilty about neglecting his job and threatening his family's financial security. If he spends less time at home and more at the office, he feels guilty about neglecting the emotional needs of his wife and family. Either way he is trapped.

It is important to note that a wife's complaint may be legitimate if her husband has been using his overtime as means of escaping the family, but in this case Mary is attempting to control her husband's use of time to prove that "you belong to me."

Why does one need to encourage separate interests with an intimate? One basic scientific truth in psychology is that each person is a unique human being with inherited talents and abilities which may be developed in interaction with the environment. When persons experience progress with the development of their talents, they will find fulfillment and create a happier intimacy. However, because we are different persons, separate interests do exist. So mates naturally have interests which do not include each other.

Sometimes women are at a disadvantage in developing their interests because of a sense of responsibility to mate, children, and domestic duties. These areas of responsibility may never disappear, and if a woman does not *take* time to develop her interests, time will rarely be available.

Men also easily become trapped by job responsibilities, so that they find it difficult to squeeze out time for separate interests. Yet rarely does a job demand that all one's talents be used. Outside interests are needed for talents not to lie dormant, or atrophy. My advice to both sexes is to *decide* to take time for interests you enjoy. If you wait for magic to provide you with time, it will never be available.

Separate Friends

Another act of possessiveness is a subtle (or not-so-subtle) attack on an intimate's friends. For example, Joan has a group of friends with whom she plays bridge every Wednesday. Her husband makes fun of the women and the value of their gatherings. He is trying to cut his wife's ties of friendship so that she will "belong" more completely to him. Actually, these efforts are largely unconscious. However, until he recognizes the process of possessiveness and works to resolve it, he will continue to find reasons to oppose her friendships.

Persons who see their mates as a possession may not understand friendships—however platonic—outside of marriage. Somehow, from the point of view of the possessor, outside relationships are considered an act of disloyalty toward the intimacy. This is especially true if sexual infidelity is involved.

Loyalty in intimacy is too often defined narrowly as sexual fidelity, yet sexual fidelity may or may not be involved with loyalty in a relationship. When one mate says to another, "I trust you to be loyal," this can mean, "I trust you to be concerned with what is good for the relationship, and to consider my growth needs as important as your own." Such a definition places loyalty where it belongs—in the context of the quality of a relationship between two persons.

Since caring means supporting the growth of an intimate, that support will be given even when one is threatened by the consequences of a mate's growth. The wife of a friend of mine spent six weeks at a university in another state, receiving special training as a music therapist for children with emotional problems. This man admitted a sense of being unhappy at the separation since he knew he would be lonely without her. But his caring for her was more important to him than his unhappiness. Loyalty here meant support for his wife's development as a teacher. Disloyalty would have meant putting his immediate needs ahead of his wife's growth and development. He was helped by a knowledge that any friendships she made during the separation would not replace him in the relationship. Even if one is not sure, the fear of replacement can be openly expressed and discussed.

If one partner is genuinely threatened by the possibility of sexual involvement between an intimate and an outside friend, feelings need to be openly discussed between the two partners. Misunderstandings can be brought out in the open and fears usually alleviated by communication. Or, if there is enough threat to the intimacy from a friendship and the threat cannot be sufficiently reduced by discussion, a mate can consider a change in the friendship. When the value of a primary intimacy and the value of a friendship are weighed, a choice is sometimes necessary, but such cases which involve an either/or choice are the exception.

Because of the limitations of time and energy as well as social conditioning, it is difficult to maintain multiple sex relationships simultaneously without taking away from the primary intimacy. If relationships outside of one's marriage or intimacy tend to replace the intimacy between partners, the question of loyalty to the intimacy is a legitimate one.

Caring for persons outside of marriage, however,

does not have to take away *per se* from caring for one's marital partner. Where friendships with either sex outside of marriage are concerned, we probably have all learned from experience—whether we like to admit it or not—that loving one person does not prevent our caring for others. It may, in fact, make loving others easier.

Unfortunately, friendships with the opposite sex are usually suspected of being affairs. This tragic situation, which is a regression to the time when boys played with boys and girls played with girls, must be eliminated.

A caring, heterosexual relationship can evolve a unique pattern of its own, particular to the two persons involved, and enrich other intimacies. If marriage becomes the end of caring relationships with *either* sex outside of the marriage itself, it will become an emotional dead end where growth stops and sterility begins. Putting an end to friendships with the opposite sex because of marriage does not increase the commitment to a primary intimacy, but cuts off meaningful encounters with half of the population. By our definition of loyalty, putting an end to extramarital friendships is a disloyal act, as it is not in the interest of either mate.

I know of a husband and wife who have friends of the opposite sex—some they enjoy together, some they enjoy separately. This couple relates to each other, and to outside friends, as person to person. I have not noticed seductive behavior or "sex games" going on in their outside relationships, but if sex did occur with any of their friends, I feel sure they would still relate as human beings. Neither has any doubts about the commitment to the primary relationship between them, or that it is first in their lives. Yet there is room for meaningful friendships with the opposite sex, friendships which are not primarily sexual because sex is not the major reason for the friendships. And their extramarital friendships do not need sexual expression to be meaningful.

This may sound like an ideal example of a happy

marriage. You may be saying to yourself, "It's easy to avoid conflict when intimates feel the same way about separate friends." But you and your mate can move in the direction of accepting separate friends, a little at a time, and help parole each other from a social prison of your own making.

Intimacies or marriages are never really completely open or closed to mate growth, or to separate friends. Such extremes do not exist in reality. What is most important is the direction of your intimacy: whether there is movement toward better intimacy and increased capacity to tolerate separateness.

Separate Time

No intimacy can survive unless partners have some time physically apart from an intimate. Each of us needs emotional space to be with ourselves—to organize our thoughts and sort our emotions. This means that at times we will be less responsive to an intimate, and vice versa. A need for distance is normal and can be understood as such, instead of interpreted as a sign of rejection. All of us have moments when we need to be apart, and backing off in such instances is not a sign of diminished caring.

Total escape from the emotional pressure of intimacy is necessary occasionally if intimacy is to remain alive. The case of a friend illustrates this. A woman with four children, a demanding job, and membership in several clubs was beginning to feel so pressured emotionally that she was making life uncomfortable for those around her. She told her husband that she would like to go away by herself for a few days to another city. Instead of saying, "But what about the children?" or "It isn't safe," or "I feel just as cooped up as you but I don't leave," he simply let her go, understanding her need for apartness.

She drove to a city some 150 miles away and spent

the weekend shopping, sleeping late, and relaxing. While she was reading by the pool at her hotel, another guest began a conversation with her about her book on extrasensory perception. The guest turned out to be a lawyer who was in town to work on a legal case. Their conversation became quite animated over the shared interest in ESP and it was natural for them to continue the conversation over a cocktail inside.

They shared information about their marriages and families with an openness that sometimes occurs with a stranger one will probably not see again. She paused, however, when he asked her to join him for dinner. Would she be saying "yes" to more than the meal? Reviewing the honesty of their conversation, she decided to accept. Over steak and red wine, she shared the fact that she loved her husband and children, but needed separation at times. It had not occurred to the lawyer that his wife might have some of the same needs for separation. He was grateful for the insight.

As the dinner ended, she thanked her new friend for the meal and the company, and said she wished to read for awhile. She considered it a compliment that he asked her to talk further in his room, but she did not want a closer relationship with him. A warm hug at her door when he walked her back to her room gave her a good feeling without regrets.

En route home there was no stopping along the way. She was refreshed, and as content to return as she had been eager to leave. Like Nora in Ibsen's *A Doll's House,* she realized that, in the long run, she belonged first to herself. Unlike Nora, she did not have to leave home permanently to be committed to herself.

As intimate relationships mature, mate autonomy develops until there is freedom for both to act as individuals while still being intimates. If our model for autonomy is flexible enough, it will allow both male and female to make friends separately, to have separate interests, and to have time apart to experience the aloneness that is part of the reality of being a person.

Freedom to develop—individually and together—reflects the understanding that one belongs *with* an intimate, and not *to* one. We are better able to join together in intimacy if we have experiences that remind us that we are separate persons.

The Meaning of Responsibility for Self

A central solution to the "you belong to me" fiction is a realistic look at the responsibility for self versus the responsibility for one's intimate. Since responsibility for self is within your control, realization of this lightens your load.

Responsibility for self means accepting responsibility for self-development, the quality of your existence, and your identity as a person. Responsibility for your life encompasses more than duties and obligations; it implies a state of being. Responsibility for self means a keen awareness that to live is to risk failure and success, and to understand that choices are a personal responsibility. Responsibility for self also involves the intention to be what your genetic personality and environment will allow you to be. Interestingly, as we become more responsible for ourselves we tend to shun inappropriate responsibility, such as attempts to control the life of an intimate. Accepting responsibility for self tends to relieve one of a desire to possess. There are many ways, however, how persons avoid responsibility for self.

Persons may function as responsible citizens and perform well at their jobs, but may not assume responsibility for what happens to them. Or they may let others make their decisions, or decide for themselves according to group norms, or refuse to decide at all.

Some persons protect themselves by refusing to take a position on issues or to give a response that is truly individual. By equivocal answers such as "It could be this—or that," by waiting to agree with the group, or by using generalizations, truisms and cliches, they avoid an authentic response.

Fear of being a person and assuming responsibility for oneself inevitably frustrates an intimate. An intimate will never be sure where he/she stands, since the person in question does not want the responsibility of a personal choice which involves self-exposure.

Consider the predicament of a female patient who, after six months of psychotherapy, desired a more personal relationship with her husband. Communication from him had been superficial and impersonal so that she never knew where he stood.

His passivity had been less threatening, even desirable, to her before her therapy. Because of a dominating father who had terrified her as a child, she had been afraid of men. She had equated femininity with being vulnerable and dominated, as her mother had been. As psychotherapy helped her to understand and deal with her fear of her father, she began to change. The status quo of her marital relationship was upset, and she now needed more from her husband as a person.

Although defensive and feeling threatened by her challenge, he decided to enter psychotherapy. An exploration of his past revealed that his mother had leaned on him heavily after a divorce from his father when he was five years old, and controlled him by the theme, "You are responsible for my happiness." Because his mother was never really happy, he felt that he was a failure. He closed the door on his feelings and kept his relationships impersonal and formal.

After he established a relationship of confidence with the therapist, he gradually began to detect underlying feelings of all kinds: love, hate, anger, envy, and hopelessness. It took months of hard therapeutic work before he began to communicate with his wife. But as he came to know himself better, he was better able to take a stand and accept responsibility. He emerged as a more distinct individual.

As he asserted himself, his wife reacted with some anxiety, until she realized that he was different from her father. In spite of what she thought was her readiness to accept change in him, she had to learn to be at ease with his strength as a male. She had to deal more directly with his likes and dislikes, which, in turn, meant confrontation.

As he assumed responsibility for his life and abilities, he realized that his job did not draw on his basic talents or provide him with inner satisfaction. After much deliberation, he quit his job and returned to college to complete a degree in a field that interested him. His wife went to work to support the two of them, planning to return to school later herself.

By becoming more accepting of and comfortable with himself, he defeated his basic source of anxiety: fear of accepting responsibility for being himself.

Out of Possessiveness to Trust

One important way to defeat the "you belong to me" fiction is to care for and trust yourself. The intention to move in this direction starts the process of change. As self-trust increases, the sense of insecurity decreases, and there is less need to build fences around an intimate. Self-trust precedes genuine self-caring. Observation in psychotherapy indicates that the experience of self-trust is gradual, almost imperceptible, until a person feels that his or her essential being or person is good. Anxiety decreases, and self-confidence increases. Deep down the awareness grows that even the most misdirected patterns have a positive basis.

As self-trust develops, a person becomes less defensive and more open. The trust I am talking about here goes deeper than trusting what a person will do. Trusting oneself and one's intimate involves a basic attitude toward people.

Carl Rogers' studies of individuals undergoing in-depth psychotherapy indicate that those who are growing more in the direction of learning to care for the self learn to trust and value the process which *is* the self.

Rogers calls this development "becoming the self which one truly is," and describes the process as follows:

> It seems to mean that the individual moves toward *being*, knowingly and acceptingly, the process he inwardly and actually *is*. He moves away from being what he is not, from being a facade. He is not trying to be more than he is, with the attendant feelings of insecurity or bombastic defensiveness. He is not trying to be less than he is, with the attendant feelings of guilt or self-depreciation. He is increasingly listening to the deepest recesses of his physiological and emotional being, and finds himself increasingly willing to be, with greater accuracy and depth, that self which he most truly is.*

Trusting the basic soundness of the human personality, a soundness which is observed when a sense of acceptance is felt, is essential not only for change but also if possessiveness is to be countered.

Homework for Intimates

What specifically can you do to work through possessive tendencies?

1. Avoid acting on your tendency to possess an intimate by being aware of it.

When an intimate meets your needs, you want to protect the "system" that supplies you. As you give with love, you seem to lose a part of yourself. A part of you is with the loved intimate. Fear of potential loss of self, then, may become possessiveness.

It may seem too idealistic to expect human beings to give themselves in love and not attach some strings. Yet, loving with few strings is more likely to keep loving intact. As we experience the rewards of better intimacy

---

* *On Becoming a Person*, pp. 175–176.

without the attitude of "you belong to me," the fears of losing an intimate will diminish.

Our potential to be nonpossessive has a parallel in theology, where God, in love, provided us with individuality and free will, and risked our rejection. Would God create free choice and all that goes with it—the defeats and lost love—if the odds were not heavily on the side of our choosing eventually to be in relationship with Him and each other?

We may resist working against possessiveness because we lack conviction that it is self-defeating, and ultimately defeats intimacy. Instead, we often feel that *not* being possessive will give an intimate permission to leave the relationship. We may even tell a mate that being possessive means we "really care."

To summarize: In order to eliminate possessiveness and move toward the freedom of nonpossessiveness, we need first to be convinced that possessiveness defeats intimacy, and that the odds are better that intimacy will remain enjoyable as we give it up.

2. Recognize that the quality of an intimate relationship is the basis for security.

If we accept this assumption, we will see that security in a relationship where intimates "belong" to each other is pure illusion. Security is enhanced when we relate to our intimates in ways which enhance their growth and ours. When communication is an ongoing reality, when acceptance of the other person is practiced, and when two intimates have fun together, there is an objective basis to feel secure. Caring for the well-being of one's intimate as much or more than one's own well-being creates a secure relationship.

3. Encourage separate friends and interests. (You will not lose an intimate; you will find a more enriched intimacy.)

As you study your intimate's talents and abilities, encourage situations where they can be developed. Affirm your intimate's right to have friends of either sex, and your intimacy will gain.

Let me illustrate the above points by an example of

a man who encouraged his mate to return to school to complete her bachelor's degree, take art lessons to better develop her artistic talent, and bring friends home that seemed to contribute to her growth.

He did this with some threat to himself, since her going back to school involved lunch with fellow students, male and female, and friendships with several professors. But he definitely decided that he, as well as she, would reap the benefits.

The art lessons also caused a minor problem because the male mate was used to his intimate being available most of his nonwork hours. When she painted for several hours in a room reserved for her art, and went to a weekly art lesson, he would feel "left out" and "deserted." He liked to have her available when he wanted her. And that was the exact problem with the old way: without realizing it, he had started to treat his intimate as an object to be available on his terms. He had taken for granted how she habitually met his needs.

His basis for a change in attitude consisted of a commitment to her welfare, which included her right to pursue an interest he would not be a part of. Her enthusiasm for art spilled over into the relationship, and he felt enriched by the vitality. In addition, he learned from her new perceptions. He had never realized the many aspects of light and color that existed, and as he listened to what she had learned he began to see more in the world about him.

Yes, separate friends and interests can be threatening. Yet some reminders to yourself may help lessen the threat you feel. Remember that

- You cannot be all things to your mate.
- Your caring for your mate, if it is caring, must include growth friendships which he/she enjoys.
- Your intimate is, and will continue to be, happy, because he/she is developing individual interests.

Some threats will always remain with us as we encourage separateness, but the result will be better intimacy. As we really accept the premise that "the stronger and more fulfilled an intimate, the better the intimacy," we will be on our way toward freedom from posssssiveness.

Will a movement toward a more open relationship, where separate friends and interests exist, create a distance in intimacy? This is a common fear, but intimacy is best when intimates vary emotional distance. However, if intimacy is already in dire need of repair, and the principles of good and growing intimacy discussed in other chapters are not being followed, separate friends and interests alone will not solve the intimacy problem. Each individual may feel better, but there is no substitute, for example, for specific work with communication.

Relinquishing the fiction of "you belong to me" raises the probability that two intimates can develop toward autonomy and still experience an alive, enjoyable intimacy.

* * *

In sustained intimacy, and especially in marriage, our learned tendency to want an intimate to "belong to us" is intensified because of feelings of dependency and vulnerability. Because of our fears, the fiction that "you belong to me" will not be dislodged easily. But we can be helped not to act out the fiction by 1) becoming aware of our feeling, and 2) affirming ourselves as persons of worth. Then we will be free to move toward increased self-trust and more nonpossessive caring for our intimate.

The combination which assures intimacy with regard for separateness is the formula: $A + C = Ei$. This means that *autonomy* plus *collaboration* equals *enriched intimacy* between intimates. Autonomy is necessary for intimacy; otherwise, the very intensity of intimacy would seem to absorb our identity as persons. Only when we do not belong to each other can we really risk being intimate and maintain our separate identity.

Being possessive not only cripples the growth of the possessed and places a heavy burden on the possessor, but also decreases the satisfaction within the intimacy itself. And increased satisfaction in intimacy—not belonging to one another—is really our goal.

9 | *Love Without Terms Is a Gift Without Strings*

How well can you take a feeling of rejection from someone you love? If your answer is "not well," you are like most persons, and you will tend to use "love on my terms" without realizing it. "Love on my terms" is a defense against rejection, and a major problem in intimacy, since overtures of love are exposed daily to rejection.

Fear of rejection and its resulting emotional pain lead to patterns of manipulation and control. Fearing vulnerability, we give in to or acquire these patterns of behavior which keep us from being known. The less known we are, the more effective our manipulation, but the more self-defeating our attempts to be loved.

If personified, these patterns might be called

- the moralist—
- the doormat—
- the promoter—
- the negotiator—
- the buyer—
- the withholder.

Each of these says, "Love will be given on my terms." Understanding how these aspects of our personalities function can help us to love and be loved in a straight-forward way. "Love on my terms" is a destructive fiction because love is squelched in efforts to control love input/output. True intimacy exists in direct, non-manipulatory giving and receiving.

The Moralist

The moralist in us expects to earn love by doing all the "right" things. Hounded by the "oughts" and "shoulds" of life, this side of us sincerely attempts to be virtuous, kind, considerate—the "model" husband or wife. Duty and obligation are elevated to a place of prime importance, and judgment is rendered when a mate does not perform according to expectations.

Our moralist is thoroughly convinced that deeds—keeping the house spotless, the yard mowed, or the garden planted—fulfill the marriage contract. Marriage on such a basis becomes a grim business of "doing duties." Person-to-person communication is neglected and family fun postponed indefinitely as family chores take top priority. Moralizing leads us to

—punish a mate for neglecting family duties, since failure to perform appears as a grievous fault and evidence of "not caring."
—feel martyred, suffering "virtuously" for the sake of the mate, if we perform and the mate does not.

Love and affection are expected as rewards for performance, and given when "earned" by following the rules.

Feeling martyred, we might say: "I have been working all day for you and the kids; the least I can expect is . . .", or "I always think of your feelings and try to please you."

From our judgmental stance we might say: "Shouldn't

you have done the dishes by now?" or "You never spend enough time at home."

In moralizing we are not only recreating negative parental patterns, but we are also striving to reduce feelings of inadequacy. Somehow feeling that we are not "good" enough drives us to excessive efforts to do the "right" thing as proof that we deserve love. This pattern is emotionally contagious and usually arouses inadequacy feelings in our mate. As a result, he or she may react by

—trying to earn our love in return,
—giving love with a forced quality and resenting it,
—giving up entirely the effort to love.

Authentic love is not a conditioned response to virtuous behavior. While the moralist is saying to the mate, "After all I've done, you should love me," the message being heard is, "Look how virtuous I am; your response is earned, not given." Such an attitude robs the giver of his gift.

The moralist in us tells us to govern our behavior and to control that of others by referring to a set of rules established either by parents or society. Religious teachings also may be used as a club to hit those who offend. The payoff is an escape from responsibility for making decisions on the basis of what is right at that time, in that situation, and for the specific individuals involved.

How can one work to change the pattern of the moralist within? First, by making a conscious decision to change, since a decision made releases forces in us which pave the way for change. Specific steps are suggested:

• Start admitting mistakes. If you can't find any, ask someone for help.
• Stop accusing your mate of "bad" behavior and look at yourself, not just your performance. Stop accusing, period.

- Accept your mistakes; it will help you to accept your partner's. Tolerance starts at home.
- Express feelings (hurt, rejection, warmth). You are not a machine!
- Place fewer controls on yourself; trust yourself more. It's exciting to take some risks.
- Be responsible for your decisions. You'll feel more grown-up.
- Relax; stop fighting things! Give yourself A's for relaxation.
- Stop robbing your mate of credit for giving; love cannot be earned. Receiving is fun, too!

The Doormat

The doormat within us attempts to win affection by being overly permissive and by appealing to our mate's narcissism and self-interest. The doormat wants to grant every whim, and seldom utters the word "no."

When we allow our doormat to take over, we are again escaping responsibility for our actions, even our very existence. Such statements as "Whatever you want is all right with me" place responsibility for decision-making on the mate, the payoff being that if something goes wrong, the mate will get the blame. We can then say, "You made the decision, not I."

Such behavior may seem virtuous and loving; it's as if we were saying, "Do what you will, I will still love you." In reality, the pattern is self-defeating, since over-indulgence may produce a tryant who becomes progressively less able to love. As the tyrant loses respect and withdraws further, the doormat in us may then counter with, "Even though you don't love me, I will still love you." What a payoff in control that is! By "heaping coals of fire" upon his head, we are able to manipulate through guilt.

Actually, if we attempt to extract love by

- being overly submissive—
- allowing or encouraging our mate to dominate us—
- giving up personal freedom—
- sacrificing human dignity—

to "earn" love, the satisfaction of martyrdom or whatever affection may result is not worth the price. By refusing to be individuals, we make it difficult for a mate to give affection.

If you recognize strong doormat tendencies within you, think about the following ways of effecting change:

- Search out differences between you and your mate; point them out verbally.
- Think through your ideas; assert them.
- Express your feelings more. To do so doesn't require a fund of information.
- Challenge your mate, even if conflict ensues.
- Refuse to be mistreated; do not back down!
- Don't be nice at the expense of being honest.
- Be responsible for your actions.

When your doormat threatens to swallow you, ask yourself these questions:

- What is wrong with an honest difference of opinion between husband and wife?
- Are you afraid of your own anger? your mate's anger?
- Is it possible for two entirely separate individuals to agree on every issue?
- Is it sensible or advisable for one to be submissive to the other on the basis of sex?

Isn't it good news to know that you may be more easily loved when you accept responsibility, challenge your mate, and take a stand?

The Promoter

The promoter in us attempts to sell an image of the self in return for "payola" in the form of sex, special favors, or other indulgences. The chart below illustrates some promotional patterns.

Image Promoted	Actual Behavior
Hardworking businessman attending night meetings	Is entertained at night
Good money manager	Controls money for self-indulgence
Charitable giver, exhausted from meeting the demands of others	Allows no time to relate to intimate
Considerate spouse	Makes a token show of consideration
Able decision-maker	Rarely accepts mate's ideas
Hardworking homemaker	Watches soap operas, gossips, talks on telephone excessively

If our promoter is successful, we can actually brainwash our partners into thinking our way is advantageous. By presenting a favorable image, we risk little while appearing to show affection. What the real self feels is rarely revealed, since self-revelation would remove our mask and give us away.

A personality dominated by the promoter pattern is frequently successful in the business world, where much time and effort are spent on a carefully constructed image. Such an image, although successful in the outside world, will rarely hold up in marriage. The marital partner is the hardest client to sell, since after a period of several years the spouse knows the person beneath the facade.

The realization that everybody buys except those who know us best will be quite depressing to our promoter.

If we are accustomed to receiving a favorable response from people at work or in social situations, a negative response at home will be hard to take. If the sales pitch is turned down with regularity, there will be a temptation to take the promotions elsewhere.

The first step in checkmating the promoter in us is to realize that the pattern is bankrupt and self-defeating. Underlying feelings of inadequacy, which are often the dynamic behind promotion, can be dealt with if we make a decision to

- Share fears and insecurities with someone close and try to understand whether the basis for them is justifiable.
- Ask associates how we really come across. We may not be fooling anyone!
- Quit trying to sell an image of ourselves, and be as real as possible.

Facing feelings of insecurity will help us turn off the promoter. The combination of awareness of the inner promoter and an increasing ability to be ourselves will enable us to give and receive love more effectively.

The Buyer

The buyer's method of attempting to get love is probably the most easily recognizable. After attempting to purchase love with a shower of gifts, our buyer cries, "Why don't you love me after all I've given you?" The gifts may be ostentatious ones, such as a car, a fur coat, a diamond ring; or they may be more practical presents, such as an electric toaster or a new wallet. Even more subtle, they may be sentimental items, such as a single rose. Whatever the gift, the aim is to make the recipient feel both positive and indebted toward the giver.

"Not O.K." feelings of unworthiness have convinced those of us dominated by the buyer pattern that we cannot be loved for ourselves alone. Fearing rejection, we fear giving ourselves and substitute objects instead. Our buyer confirms our fears, whispering, "As long as I give my mate every luxury, I won't have to make an emotional commitment." We forget that nobody likes to feel "bought"—that although it is pleasant to receive gifts, the recipient is likely to become resentful when impersonal, inanimate objects are consistently substituted for the gift of self.

One woman had an insatiable need to give presents to friends, relatives, and her husband. At Christmas her budget was strained to the breaking point, and she had to borrow money to pay for gifts. The compulsive nature of her buying indicated that she needed to prove she cared, and believed that she would lose affection if intimates were not obligated by gifts. Her buyer told her, "No one will love you if you don't give them presents."

What can you do when the buyer in you persuades you that by giving "things" you can expect affection in return? You can remember that

- warmth—
- acceptance—
- understanding—
- time—
- consideration—

are not for sale, nor bought at any price, but you can give (and get!) them. Valuing ourselves makes it possible to recognize that others value us, not for the material gifts we can give, but for the gift of ourselves.

After all, only *persons* can meet human needs.

The Negotiator

Sometimes under the guise of give-and-take, we use negotiations, or an exchange of favors, to control an intimate.

The arrangement may be something like this: "If

you'll buy me this new dress, I'll be more interested in sex"; or, "I won't spend as much time on the golf course if you won't ask me to help around the house."

An exchange of favors and a degree of compromise is desirable in every relationship. But what distinguishes negotiation from compromise is the motivation behind the bargaining. When giving is done in order to receive, the enjoyment of giving is sacrificed. Our negotiator warns us to examine every transaction for equality in giving and receiving—as if a scale existed to measure giving!

An impersonal and dehumanizing element pervades the core of a relationship when our negotiator takes over, and bargaining becomes the major way of relating.

Negotiations suggest the presence of warring factions or conflicting interests. If caring is our objective, and we want to work with our mate, alternative patterns do exist. Whenever we are tempted to negotiate to get our way, we can

- Think of the ways our mate gives to us.
- Think of the pleasure we experience when our mate gives unexpected support, unsolicited compliments, or spontaneous gifts.
- Think of ways we can give spontaneously.
- Refuse to feel rejected if our mate doesn't respond to our gift.
- Realize that each person needs to give in a way that is comfortable for him.
- Explain to our mate how we wish to receive, and what we want.

Try this exercise:

Picture in your mind a scene where you give your mate a gift he/she likes, such as a necktie or flowers. Your mate smiles politely, but without enthusiasm, and offers you little affection in return. How do you feel about the response? hurt? disappointed? angry? all three?

Face the feeling. Can you survive a lack of response to your giving?

Repeat the same scene with a more personal gift, such as a show of physical affection. Your mate pulls away. Visualize this in detail. Now, how do you feel? Can you survive the rejection? You don't like it, but you are able to work through your disappointment.

Fear of rejection often paralyzes the process of giving. Facing the thing feared most—rejection—allows one to become desensitized to rejection and to gain confidence that giving need not be dependent on a response. Confidence comes with a sense of independence in giving. Realization that giving is its own reward is a step toward more personal freedom to give, and builds emotional maturity.

Negotiations are usually self-protective. By working on desensitizing ourselves we are strengthened in our ability to give without the imagined protection of a "bargain."

To negotiate is to rob oneself of the pleasures of real giving.

The Withholder

Withholding is a power tool in an intimate relationship. Sometimes our withholder works hand in hand with our negotiator. For example, if a negotiation is rejected, we may become withholders, not only withdrawing the original offer, but withholding something in addition. Favorites for withholding are

- sex—
- time—
- conversation—
- attention—
- compliments—
- help.

The payoff? Control, of course.

Withholding is a favorite device of the supposedly

"weaker" or more submissive member in the relationship. This partner, instead of making demands, chooses a more passive, less direct method of manipulation to get "love on my terms." By depriving the mate of something desired, the withholder in us may be

- manipulating the mate into wooing us,
- avoiding involvement,
- paying back a mate for disappointments or for real or imagined injuries.

Take the case of Kay. She expected her husband to do many of the things her father did before they married, such as buy license plates, take the car to the shop, make minor repairs at home, and watch the budget. She was disappointed when her husband did none of these, but expected her to do them. She hit back by withholding where she knew it would hurt most: in physical affection. Actually, he learned nothing this way, but became more resentful, and began to have business meetings at night.

When the expectations of each were clarified in psychotherapy and when compromise decisions were reached, the communication impasse was resolved. Kay learned to do more for herself, and in so doing, received more mate support. She also learned to vocalize anger when it occurred instead of withholding affection.

What can you do to discourage your withholder from taking control?

- Look for your own contribution to marital problems, asking, "How have I been unloving at home?"
- Consider whether your expectations for your mate are realistic and appropriate.
- Listen when your mate has a criticism.
- Admit your hurt feelings and disappointments; they will occur.
- Accept your spouse's response to you.

- Consider whether the power you seem to get by withholding is worth the payoff. Real power is in giving.
- Think about the rewards you receive when you give.

*   *   *

When we inventory the contributions to intimacy of

- the moralist—
- the doormat—
- the promoter—
- the buyer—
- the negotiator—
- the withholder—

we find that we are short-changing ourselves and our mate if we allow any of these to become a predominant pattern in our intimate relationships. Each is an expression of the desire for "love on my terms," an attitude which stresses the *control* of love, rather than the *development* of love.

Beneath these love control techniques lies the implied threat that love in intimacy is dangerous—dangerous because we are dependent on our mate to meet essential emotional needs. When we are more able to love actively without being dependent on the response of our intimate, we will be less security-conscious about receiving love. The results are:

- Freedom to love in place of fear,
- Growth in love in place of restrictions on love,
- Confidence to love in a world of uncertainty.

We can be loved on *our* terms when the "our" involved is that of two people striving to be authentic with each other. No formal arrangement, no "negotiated contract" is necessary, just an understanding in which each partner is allowed to give according to his or her own personality. The development of love without terms—a gift without strings, not dependent on being received—strengthens us to give with greater conviction and commitment.

10 | Change Is the Name of the Game with Intimate Relationships

The illusion that "our love will not change" teaches the misleading lesson that personality is static, and that intimacy stands still. But personality does change, and two growing personalities create an intimacy that moves through stages of change.

Accepting these two concepts alone would release intimates from a fiction that provides a false sense of security, guarantees later disappointment, and prevents preparation for the natural developments that occur within intimacy.

In order to test what you know about change in personalities and sustained intimate relationships, try to answer the fifteen questions below:

TRUE FALSE

1. When the first child is born, a marital crisis occurs.
2. After children grow up and leave home, there is less reason for a couple to stay together.
3. Couples have a natural tendency to withdraw from social contact in later years.
4. Getting to know a partner in early marriage usually brings about some disillusionment.

164

TRUE FALSE

5. A major reevaluation of life usually occurs after age forty.

6. Admitting mistakes is essential in marriage.

7. The seventh-year crisis in marriage requires that dreams be given up for reality.

8. If a couple is skilled, "courtship" as a stage can go on forever.

9. After age sixty, the sexual side of marriage is over.

10. Arguments should be avoided to preserve marital harmony.

11. Romantic illusions help maintain an alive marriage.

12. After the first five years of life, little personality change is possible.

13. Personality is established by age twenty-one with few changes after that.

14. Self-actualized persons are often unrealistic.

15. A strong sense of the self is characteristic of a self-actualized person.

The above questions involve basic issues concerning change in personality and intimacy. The first seven statements are true, the next seven false, and the last one true.

Learning to Expect Change

How can we prepare ourselves for the changes that will inevitably occur in ourselves and our mate?

Two persons in love often expect their relationship not to change after they marry. Most intimates also have the notion, largely unconscious, that their partner will not change. What a trap intimacy becomes when a "contract" exists that the individuals, and the form of intimacy, will not change!

These "no change" attitudes are destructive to individual personality and will result in a dead relationship. Whether persons are able to become themselves or grow in the direction of what they were created to be is, to a degree, dependent on the attitudes of those close to them. Our influence is never neutral; we either help or hinder our intimate.

What is needed by intimates is a commitment to enhance the growth in the relationship. If there is a single issue crucial to the removal of intimacy fictions, this is it. Two of my friends were married recently in a ceremony designed by themselves and their pastor. Part of the ceremony went like this: "I, Tom, promise not to block your growth, but to help you develop in any way I can." In turn, Beth vowed to support Tom's growth. They both agreed to help each other through the inevitable changes in their relationship. In this situation there is a conscious avoidance of the fiction that intimates will not change, and a commitment to assist one's spouse in the process of change.

In my opinion this attitude is dramatically different from the way most persons enter marriage or intimacy. To those who fear that a spouse's commitment to growth will encourage early termination of the marriage, I suggest the contrary. Intimacy prospers when intimates are committed to growth. Even if the relationship ends sooner from such a growth commitment, the time spent in the relationship will be decidedly more fulfilling.

You may wonder whether my sample of persons is representative of the population at large. Yes and No. Persons who seek a psychotherapist for help in problems of living are different in that they are usually more motivated than others to learn to solve their dilemmas. Yet overall, these persons are like you and me, and go through experiences common to all of us.

Accepting the idea that personality *does* change would revolutionize intimacy. But agreeing to this idea with your intellect may be a far cry from accepting it emotionally. To achieve emotional acceptance of an idea one must be actively involved in the process of learning. Let's work with the idea of change in your mate to see how prepared you are for change.

Try to picture your intimate behaving differently in several ways. If he/she is quiet, somewhat reserved, and seldom the cause of emotional ripples, envision your mate as more outspoken, more assertive, more involved in controversial exchanges. How do you feel about these changes? How do you imagine that you would respond to these changes? Your feelings may tell you more about your reaction than your imagination.

If the thought of your mate being more outgoing and outspoken is threatening, admit it, but do not stop there. What is the threat? Can you accept your mate's becoming stronger as a person, and perhaps stronger in the relationship? Threat, fear, feelings of inadequacy, and low self-confidence are all emotions which breed resistance to change in an intimate. But you and your mate *can* deal with honest feelings about change.

If these emotions are not faced, they will be expressed in camouflaged form to the destruction of alive intimacy. You need not be ashamed of these feelings. Let the idea soak in that there is no emotion you need be ashamed of, or should avoid confronting. An intimate who denies emotions within himself endangers the life of an intimacy. So we see that the basis for coping with change is to *accept* our feelings in response to mate changes. This attitude creates a climate for self-growth.

Assisting Self-Change

There is a definite correlation between resistance to mate growth and resistance to self-growth. Change in your mate will seem less threatening if you are open to self-change in a direction consistent with your personality.

We have stressed the importance of dealing with our

own emotions and those of our intimate. How we deal with our emotions is a guide to our emotional maturity. And emotional maturity is a basis for self-change, regardless of the pattern a unique personality takes.

The research of psychologist Carl Rogers in psychotherapy* shows that a person in transition toward emotional maturity tends to become more expressive, more honest about emotions, more independent, and more inclined to want to communicate. A higher degree of emotional maturity is indicated by a willingness to accept responsibility—first, for what is happening, and second, for one's feelings.

By contrast, a person who is emotionally immature tends to blame externals for what happens.

"No matter what I do ..."

"Every time I try to ..."

"It always happens to me ..."

Blaming others for feelings is a reflection of a lower degree of emotional maturity:

"You make me angry when you ..."

"I wouldn't feel this way if you wouldn't ..."

As we grow in maturity, we begin to "own" feelings, in the sense of accepting them as personal reactions and taking responsibility for them. Instead of placing the blame on external events or persons, we accept responsibility for actions and reactions:

"I get angry." (Instead of "You make me angry.")

"I realize how I close people out by being irritable." (Instead of "People seem to avoid me.")

In accepting responsibility for actions and feelings, we experience a heightened sense of self in all situations. This sense of self does much to cut through feelings of inadequacy. As we reach higher levels of emotional maturity, we tend to experience all feelings immediately. This is a sign that we are in touch with the inner self. Inevitably this "being in touch emotionally" involves caring and acceptance of one's self.

"I really like myself now."

_____

* *On Becoming a Person* (Boston: Houghton Mifflin, 1961).

"I experience warm feelings toward myself."

"I feel close to myself now, like an old friend that has come back from a long journey."

Research indicates that when we reach a high level of emotional growth, where in-depth self-acceptance occurs, the change is irreversible. Instead of finding a part of ourselves unacceptable when we journey to find ourselves, we discover only a human being within. The "undesirable" aspects we hide from the outside world are only products of our fear to be ourselves. Through self-acceptance we experience a genuine caring for our "selves" which removes self-alienation. By "self" I mean a composite of ideas, feelings, and actions organized around a unique identity.

In this process of self-discovery, or literally coming to experience ourselves, we realize that personality is dynamic and changing, a process of energy that is never static.

It is interesting to see the overlap between Rogers' list of characteristics of emotional maturity and Maslow's description of persons who are highly actualized. Self-actualized persons generally have an orientation toward reality (a tendency to see things as they are); acceptance of self, others, and the world without condition; spontaneity of emotional expression; and a strong sense of self, or personal identity.

Change in the direction of self-actualization can help intimacy. As a person develops a stronger sense of self, he/she moves toward autonomy and independence, which is another characteristic of highly actualized persons. But an intimate who resists change and feels threatened by a more actualized mate can destroy intimacy altogether. If increased independence is steadfastly opposed by a mate, a more actualized person is likely to fight back and refuse to preserve a relationship that demands sacrifice of self and self-development.

No relationship is so harmonious that persons do not need to take different stands at times so that two separate human egos can exist and love together. A growing person is more likely to feel the flames of love than is one who resists change, yet the independence which comes with personality growth is easily misunderstood as less caring.

One patient became concerned that his wife was moving away from him, because of her interest in Muscular Dystrophy and the fact that she had two female friends whe were extremely close to her. He sensed her involvement in a purpose outside the family, and was aware that she shared her feelings and thoughts with close friends. Yes, she was moving, but not away from him.

Actually, she loved him at a deeper level, but her love was more far-ranging now and included a segment of mankind that needed help. She depended less on him for decisions about her life, and generally became more self-directed. With her growth, the form of love in their relationship changed from one of dependency toward one of more mutuality and interdependency. Actually, she could like her spouse better and not feel the underlying resentments usually directed at a person one depends on. And she liked herself better. She could now give more freely to her spouse as a full partner in intimacy.

Once the spouse became aware of what the change in the relationship was all about, he chose to reap the benefits for himself. He realized that she seemed to better understand his work commitments and his time spent with friends. And she greeted him with more inner joy than before. He noticed that she could give him a lift and raise his morale, while before she tended to "pull and tug" with subtle demands he could not meet. He benefited directly from her changes.

Individual personality growth is a fact of life, and this growth, or the lack of it, crucially affects the quality of intimacy.

Intimacy itself is a third reality, which has a history apart from the history of two individuals, and which at any time is heavily influenced by the degree of resolution of past crises. An awareness of typical crisis periods in intimacy and a look at ways of resolving the crises can help persons accept changes and enjoy intimacy more.

Critical Stages in Intimacy

Intimate relationships force crises that, if not dealt with effectively at the time, cause cumulative problems at later stages. Not all of these stages occur in every relationship, nor in the time sequence described, and some stages overlap with others. But awareness is necessary if couples are to understand how to deal with each stage.

Critical stages in intimacy are:

- Termination of courtship
- Early marriage or intimacy
- The first child
- The "seven-year" crisis
- The "over-forty blues"
- The departure of children
- Free time

Termination of Courtship

"Love" in courtship (dating) is usually too plastic to be the stuff sustained intimacy is made of. Some persons equate courtship caring with love, and experience a loss of love when courtship ends. This indicates an awareness that love itself is not understood, and that what seemed to be love was an illusion. Termination of courtship can mean the end of illusions about intimacy.

Many illusions about intimacy are discussed in this book, but specifically, courtship creates the illusion that we really know each other when that is actually not the case. The romance related to a dating relationship is not on solid ground because it has not stood the test of living together over a period of time.

There is nothing wrong with romantic love as such!

The real problem lies in being able to give up courtship attitudes and work on the real problems of being and living together without losing romantic love.

If one goal of dating is to test a relationship for possible sustained intimacy, or to woo a person to accept a marriage proposal, motivation to continue romance is often lost once the goal is achieved. The artificial quality that accompanies much of dating must be lost, but some of the romantic feelings can, and need to, continue after marriage to help keep the relationship alive.

How can you help to keep romantic feelings alive as the business side of living ends courtship?

By being aware of your intimate's sensitivities

Being "tuned in" to the interest of a mate, or knowing which act or attitude arouses an affectionate response, helps keep a relationship "turned on." Because you have more knowledge than when you were dating, you have an advantage. The trick is to use your knowledge of your mate's sensitivities to keep romance alive.

By meaningful giving and receiving

How often do two persons take each other for granted after marriage! Flowers are no longer given; compliments that bring color to the cheeks of one's spouse are no longer offered.

While dating, it is difficult to know what gifts have the most meaning to an intimate. In living together we learn how to give to each other. What means love to one person may not mean love to another. A gift of perfumed after-shave lotion may mean special caring to one male, while to another it may suggest an insensitive and hasty selection.

As essential as learning to give is learning to receive gifts, whether tangible or intangible, in marriage. What good is giving if the gift is not really accepted with appreciation? Many persons have difficulty receiving from anyone, and may block intimacy by sending the message, "I don't need your gifts." Even the words "thank you" can be said with varying degrees of warmth, pleasure, and delight; or the expression may be a way of uneasily saying the socially correct things without feeling. Are you aware of how you receive from your intimate?

By maintaining open communication

During dating there is often a tendency to avoid areas of controversy and differences. Open communication, however, involves exploring the whole gamut of emotions, from anger to intense love, with no area too touchy to be discussed.

Feedback is a necessary part of open communication. Since none of us is a mind reader, we need to find out how an intimate feels about situations as they arise. By "smoking out" unexpressed feelings, we do much to keep romantic love alive in intimacy.

Ann, after two years of marriage, gradually became inhibited sexually with her husband. After much peripheral conversation, she finally expressed feelings of not being important or needed in his life. In response, he expressed the feeling of being rejected by her. His tendency to overwork at the office had been a means of escaping that feeling. By not expressing feelings or giving feedback initially, each partner had played off the other's problems until a barrier was formed between them. Because this problem was discussed in therapy shortly after it began, the resolution was rapid.

Incidents like these are so common in intimacy and marriage that it is a wonder any romantic love can survive! To nurture romantic love, communicate feelings as soon as possible, and if your spouse "holds back," keep asking for feedback until it comes.

By taking pride in appearance and grooming

Of course, it is nice to be at ease with your intimate, but going too far in that direction can result in neglect of one's physical appearance. Romantic love is often a very physical expression. Attention to grooming is another way that interest in romance is expressed.

By showing affection

Perhaps this guideline is too obvious to point out. But words of affection are not enough. Few dating relationships would survive if the amount of physical affection shown in marriage were the norm for courtship. There is a natural tendency to become preoccupied with the business side of marriage to the neglect of physical affection. Awareness of the need to counter this trend can lead to increased touching and caressing both in and out of the bedroom.

Although living together means the end of courtship as a primary way of relating, part of the courtship pattern—romance in marriage—can be kept alive if we pay attention to what nurtures romance. Romance in sustained intimacy can be more firmly grounded in reality than in dating or courtship relationships.

Early Intimacy

A second crisis occurs as a wife is confronted with the multiple demands of being a lover, companion, nurse, cook, housekeeper, teacher, and career woman, and when a husband assumes his roles as economic provider, counselor, accountant, maintenance man, companion, and paramour.

Actually the ordinary demands of early marriage are more than a superman or superwoman can perform to perfection. The lack of concrete training shows up clearly when mates try to maintain intimacy and accomplish all the tasks of living. Persons with special training in human relations often find intimacy hard to cope with. So is it surprising that the normal mate finds that the joy of intimacy experienced during dating is being drained by concerns about work, budgeting, housekeeping, and finding a place in the community? Added to this, problems of communication that have not been solved with the termination of courtship make rough sledding for intimates in the reality of marriage. Built-in expectations of how roles should be performed also enter the scene.

When early marriage problems are not resolved, they leave an endless wake of turmoil which will arouse turbulence in later stages of intimacy. Sample comments from a pair of disgruntled early marrieds are cited below. Follow the internal dialogue as it progresses:

HE: I wish she would be more responsive to me at night instead of worrying so much about what we're eating.

SHE: He doesn't show me the appreciation he used to. Now he expects me to work, cook, keep the house, *and* be his lover.

HE: She doesn't realize that I am just too tired at night to be entertaining, or to help her solve the day's problems.

SHE: He doesn't understand that I have waited all day for him to come home, and all he talks about is the people at the office.

Marital duties do interfere with intimacy. She really wants to be appreciated for what she does for him, whether she has a job or not. He finds that shifting mental gears from office to home is not easy, especially since there are few chances to work out feelings that occur during the day. Both mates need to pay attention primarily to the needs of the other, as well as to express both unpleasant as well as pleasant feelings.

During early intimacy, the capacity to take care of responsibilities and still be attentive and responsive to each other helps resolve the basic problems of this stage of intimacy. Here are some relatively simple suggestions which help intimates survive early marriage successfully.

To avoid being swallowed up by the demands of early marriage, couples might:

- Show appreciation of what each mate contributes.
- Plan time together that is work free.
- Listen to each other, instead of using each other primarily as sounding boards.

If love is alive and the intimacy is enjoyable after a year or two of marriage, then the time is right to consider another commitment: whether to have a family or not. If a child is born during the first year, critical stages may overlap. Ideally, a marriage should have a sound, long-range commitment before the birth of the first child.

The First Child

The first child's birth naturally produces changes in the husband/wife relationship. Some of these changes are critical to their intimacy. We might hear these expressions of feelings:

HE: She pays more attention to the baby than she does to me.

SHE: Why should I have to be the one that gets up at night when the baby cries?

HE: We rarely have fun anymore. If we go out, she has to call home continuously to see if the baby is all right.

SHE: He doesn't show me he cares as much as before.

The psychological impact of their first child on the parents' attitudes toward each other is often a decisive factor at this stage of marriage. When a new member is added to a group, the group itself changes. A father may feel somewhat rebuffed and left out of a close mother-infant relationship, but repressed feelings of jealousy may manifest themselves as hostilities toward his wife. Or a young wife who is not yet adjusted to the first stage of marriage, and who now has the additional responsibility of a child, may feel overburdened and express resentments toward her husband. How can this crisis be solved?

Resolution of the crisis of childbirth is greatly aided by the father's helping more. He might:

- Get up at night, alternating with his wife.
- Help with food preparation.
- Spend time with the infant.
- Support the mother emotionally as much as possible by letting her know she is still a wife/lover to him.

A wife might:

- Include her husband in child care.
- Avoid preoccupation with a child.
- Be affectionate with her husband, so that he does not associate the presence of the child with less affection for him.

If the parents work together after childbirth, the circle of love in marriage will expand to include this third person. This working together will help them resolve the crisis of a new group and deepen the marriage relationship.

The "Seven-Year Crisis"

The "seven-year crisis" may occur anywhere between the first and tenth years, i.e., whenever it is discovered that dreams must be given up for reality. It is a time for couples to take a close look at what they expect to get out of marriage and what they can give to the relationship. In all honesty, few of us are not disappointed, in some respects, with the way marriage has turned out. And we have all found something that we wish were not true about our intimates. Some of these realities we can learn to live with and accept, or we can choose to leave the relationship. Unrealistic expectations are bad bedfellows, and we need to root them out. How can we work through the "seven-year crisis"?

Give up the notion that your mate is here to live up to your image of what an ideal mate should be. You can do this by taking certain steps.

1. Expose to each other what you expected ideally.
   HE: I expected you to be turned on sexually to me all the time.
   SHE: I expected you to be a big business success.
2. Admit the anger, resentment and rage you feel because expectations have been disappointed.
   HE: I am furious at you for disappointing me.
   SHE: I hate you for letting me down and not making me feel secure.
3. Stop attempts to remake the other.
   HE: I will not accuse you of making excuses when you don't feel like having sex.
   SHE: I will not complain about not having enough money for nice clothes.
4. Admit your marital mistakes.
   HE: I have ignored you when you needed attention.
   SHE: I have withheld affection because I wanted to punish you.
   HE: I have refused to develop an interest in activities you enjoy.
   SHE: I have picked at things about you that are hard to change.
   HE: I have been too preoccupied with work.

SHE: I have expected you to make me happy without enough effort on my part.

5. Work out compromise solutions.

HE: "Where would you like to go for dinner tonight?" (I will consider what you like to do as much as I consider my own likes.)

SHE: "Would you like to visit the art museum with me and see the new exhibit?" (I will make an effort to expand my interests, and include you in them.)

HE: "May I keep the children while you do something you'd like?" (I will demand less and give more of myself.)

SHE: "Let's put the children to bed by eight so that we can have more time alone together." (I will devote more time to being alone with you.)

There is wisdom in these decisions, since mate neglect ultimately adds up to self neglect. Genuine caring for self includes equal caring for the well-being of one's mate.

A marriage at the "seven-year crisis" stage can survive if mates face disillusionment directly, admit mistakes openly and assume responsibility for them, and put a stop to efforts to fit each other into ideal images. If change does not occur at this stage, divorce or coexistence with little intimacy is a likely result.

Reevaluation After Forty

Carl Jung, the Swiss psychiatrist who was a therapist for many persons over forty, points out that a basic spirituality or inner depth may be reached at this age that can add a new dimension to marriage. However, before reaching that point, a person goes through a stage of depression and reevaluation which might be called the "over-forty blues." Symptoms of this stage are:

- Despair about commitment to a way of life that is no longer meaningful.
- Doubt that job and/or personal fulfillment goals will ever be attained.
- A shift in values which makes past accomplishments seem unimportant.
- A feeling that it is now or never to change careers.
- Concern that one will ever experience an exciting intimacy unless changes are made now.

Awareness that 1) change at this stage is desirable and that 2) the primary task is to correctly channel change helps to orient persons toward goals that fit them as individuals.

A case in point. Mr. X realized that after eighteen years as an engineer he was bored with the work and wanted to change careers. He took a battery of tests from a consulting psychologist and found out that he scored very high on personnel manager, social worker, and teacher. His scores were average on engineer, mathematician, and salesman. Personality tests showed that he was high on sociability, social presence, and poise. Drive level was high overall and emotional maturity well above average. Intelligence tests indicated superior intelligence with an excellent ability to acquire new learning.

Fortunately, Mr. X worked for a company that used psychological consultants, and it was recommended that he be transferred to personnel services. The shift was made with the attitude that both the company and Mr. X would benefit from a job change that would make the most of his talents, capabilities, and motivation.

You may wonder, what does this have to do with intimacy?

To some extent, Mr. X had taken out his job dissatisfaction at home and had become irritable and unhappy about his marriage. After he was transferred to personnel services, he became a new person at home. His happiness was contagious, and his wife felt a burden had been lifted.

The idea that one chooses a job between twenty and twenty-five and stays with this the rest of his/her life is unrealistic. Granted, in many cases change is unrealistic or impossible, but the knowledge that values and motivation may change after forty is a basis for serious contemplation of job changes. If a job change is unrealistic or impossible, a person may attempt a new approach to the same work. Special seminars or night courses may be attended, or a program of outside reading be adopted to improve current skills and develop new ones.

Practicing psychologists are capable of interpreting a battery of tests that will take the guesswork out of what type of work a person would be most successful at and like best. Some psychologists concentrate on helping persons who wish to make a transition from one field of work to another. Generally, in spite of individual limitations, some type of change or fresh approach is possible.

A major change in marriage may be appropriate at this stage as well. If a marriage which took place at age twenty-three is dead by age forty-five, couples have options to

- work toward a renewed relationship.
- accept the marriage "as is," and agree to live separate lives together.
- divorce and allow each partner to find a satisfying intimacy with someone else.

If the decision is made to develop the intimacy or revitalize the relationship, a recommitment to each other is recommended first. Creative solutions can be explored, such as the following:

- Special times can be set aside to communicate more openly and effectively.
- A plan, or plans, can be made to do something different together each week.
- New interests can be researched together, whether they involve nature, art, music, literature, the the-

ater, athletics, cooking, plants, travel, the stock market, pollution, world affairs, or the energy crisis. The main point is that the interest is new and that it is explored mutually.

• Other changes in style of living can be discussed. Intense togetherness at times and separation at other times may add new vitality to the relationship. Or separate vacations, as well as vacations together, can animate the intimacy.

Perhaps the most important element in reawakening the relationship is the first mentioned: Communication. I cannot overstress that daily communication of personal feelings has a high potential to break logjams erected over the years. Emotional communication does not happen overnight. It takes practice to get results. Listen to your feelings and practice expressing them to your intimate. Inability to understand emotion—"emotional illiteracy"—is so widespread that required courses in school are needed to alleviate the problem on a broad scale.

Divorce is another option persons may choose, especially if it appears that there is little chance for happiness in the marriage for the next thirty years. Divorce at this period is a sad experience, but a worse tragedy may be to prevent oneself or one's mate from having an alive intimacy. Divorce has been discussed in depth in another chapter, but I will say here that people are never trapped in a marriage without options unless they choose to be.

Settling for intimacy deprivation is not a positive solution. If divorce is decided against, marital partners in an intimacy-deprived relationship can agree to give each other freedom to find intimacy with other persons. This is not an easy solution and will involve many complications, but it does allow a twosome to meet intimacy needs that cannot be adequately met in the relationship.

The "over-forty reevaluation" is a crisis period full of possibilities. It is an opportunity for change that may result in a more satisfying job situation or enjoyable intimacy. If major change takes place, partners may undergo a mourning experience that is part of separation from the past. But sometimes to live in the present, it is necessary to kill the past. All of us face this challenge and the consequences of our decisions to change or not to change.

The Departure of Children

If a couple has remained together for the sake of children, a severe crisis occurs when husband and wife face what is left in the marriage after children grow up and leave home. Persons whose lives have been child-centered until now may find themselves facing a traumatic period. Unless they have developed interests of their own during the child-rearing years—club activities, volunteer work, community services, or professional careers—they are likely to find themselves faced with four decades of empty days.

It is never too late for a person to develop hobbies or learn more about any subject. Knowledge on a subject breeds new interest. It is better, of course, to develop work interests while youngsters are at home. A mother or father who is vitally interested in work or community activities is a positive influence on children, as well as a good example. In addition, children are spared the burden of feeling that they are the center of a parent's existence.

Surprisingly, the divorce rate at this stage of life is quite low. Perhaps this is because couples who grow apart during the child-rearing years now find opportunity to renew their acquaintance.

Take the case of a couple who consciously stayed together because of three children. After the last youngster left for college at age eighteen, they realized the many bonds between them. They shared a network of relationships with relatives and close friends. And the mutual interest in the lives of their children did not end when the children left home.

Somehow, they experienced a greater need for each other's companionship after the children had gone. They began to do more together, and focused less attention on offspring problems. Differences which seemed critical at earlier stages of the marriage seemed less important now.

At this point, a new commitment to intimacy is helpful if a couple wishes to stay together. If, however, there is little left of intimacy satisfaction, and no motivation to work to improve the relationship, divorce is an option. If this sounds like a simple option, it is not. Building a new life in the middle or late forties or fifties is difficult, but not impossible. I have seen persons trapped in intimacy deprivation for twenty-eight years who divorce and build a new life that has the fulfillment they missed in their marriages.

Individual attitude is the key to whether the option of divorce will lead out of deprivation to satisfaction. Negative and bitter attitudes seem to perpetuate themselves by more disappointments, while positive attitudes lead to an openness to receive intimacy satisfaction from a number of persons who are able to give it. Attitude is the key to whether divorce will make any difference.

The departure of children can signal a new life for you, either in your current intimacy or out of it toward a new one.

Free Time

After sixty-five or seventy there may be an increasing opportunity for free time, as life expectancy continues to extend well beyond the usual retirement age. New vitality must be brought into the marital relationship to combat a trend toward social isolation and low morale. Let's look at typical problems and suggestions for coping with them.

Problems	*How to Cope*
Social isolation	1. Keep in active touch with old friends. 2. Actively seek new friends of all ages. 3. Keep up social activities.
Restriction of interests	1. Try to learn about a new subject each month, by reading or observation. 2. Discuss new interests with mate and friends. 3. Share activities by attending workshops and conventions in your areas of interest.
Rigidity of habits	1. Do something different from your daily routine. 2. Vary your times for doing things (sleeping, eating, resting, playing).
A sense of lost importance	1. Offer volunteer time to charity organizations. 2. Share some parental responsibilities for grand-children, cousins, etc. 3. Make your work experience and expertise available to others in your field.
Preoccupation with self (bodily ail-ments, etc.)	1. Focus attention on others in need (nursing homes, hospital, youth homes, friends). 2. Keep as busy as your stamina will allow, mentally and physically. 3. Take better care of yourself than you did before.

All the recommendations to cope with problem patterns in the "free time" stage of marriage involve an active effort to counteract trends that seem to develop naturally. By these actions, a sense of being important as persons is affirmed. In addition, a balance between meaningful activities and activities that are sheer fun provides a full existence that enriches intimacy.

* * *

Yes, people change with time, and relationships progress through stages of change which are almost as predictable as mathematical formulae. An emotional as well as an intellectual realization of this is an essential preparation for intimates.

How well each crisis is resolved is partially a function of previous crisis resolutions. It is rarely too late to go back and review early phases of intimacy and work through problems of that stage and then progress to later stages of intimacy reevaluation.

Life itself is a learning experience full of opportunities, disappointments, crushed hopes, sublime joys, and the continual process of change that *is* the individual personality. Change is also the name of the game with intimate relationships—if we are to enjoy sustained intimacy over a lifetime.

11 | Twelve Paths to Intimacy Success

How can intimacy success be yours? Check the following questions either yes or no to see where your "IQ" (Intimacy Quotient) is.

1. Do you think that one can enjoy sustained intimacy and remain single?
2. Do you think that intimates should consider factors besides "being in love" before marriage?
3. Do you believe that your intimacy will be unique and not fit a "parental" model?
4. Do you expect to change your intimate later—to "smooth out the rough edges"?
5. Do you expect that open, emotional communication will keep your sexual relationship alive?
6. Do some intimates need to "let go" of their relationship, so that happiness may be found in another intimacy?
7. Can we retain separate identities in marriage?
8. Does continual change take place in a good intimacy?
9. Will your intimacy change, requiring reassessment of your relationship?

10. Do you think you alone can make your intimate happy?
11. Do you think love should be given without strings attached?
12. If we choose thoughtfully among the options open to us, can we anticipate joy in intimacy most of the time for most of our lives?

If you answered all the questions "yes" except for numbers 4 and 10, you scored 100%. Actually, ten correct is very good, and nine not bad. Where do you fall on the following scale?

Number Right	*"IQ"*
11–12	Very High
8–10	Above Average
5–7	Average
3–4	Below Average
1–2	Very Low

You will create, and sustain, more joy in intimacy as you move toward the correct answers to each of the twelve questions.

Simple? Yes and no. No, because it is not simple to change outmoded and destructive attitudes about intimate relationships. Yes, because once you *have* corrected misconceptions about intimacy, you will not tolerate emotional poverty for long. Higher levels of satisfaction will be yours.

How do you start the process of attitude change?

The key to beginning is C A C:

> Conviction
> Acceptance
> Communication

First, you need to be *convinced* that change or improvement is necessary. Your intimate relationship, no matter how satisfying now, is moving in either the right or wrong direction. So, as a way out of intimacy illusion, check to see that you are on the paths pointed to by the questions and explained in the preceding chapters.

Next, *accept* yourself, your intimate, and your relationship as they are now, regardless of what you want to change. Acceptance, which allows the power of love to operate, creates a situation where positive change will take place. In such an atmosphere, open, honest *communication* can happen without destructive after-effects, and intimates can listen to each other without fear and defensiveness.

The twelve paths to intimacy success can be pursued in such a way that you can bring intimacy-joy into life where this joy is missing, and sustain joy if you already have it. The paths are available to all. Let's see how these paths look so that you can find them on your own. Path one calls into question the style of intimacy, single or married, that is best for you now.

PATH ONE

Intimacy Single or Married

Does long-term intimacy, in or out of marriage, fit your personality? Being single and having satisfactory intimacy may be a more natural state, after all, for intimates. Some persons like to change a primary intimacy more often than others, and there is nothing wrong or abnormal about this.

One well-known movie star, who speaks glowingly of his ex-wife, says that he has very profound intimacies with one person at a time, and they last from one to ten years. This person dares to be different and states his position openly. There are many persons whose individual trend is to change a primary intimacy many times over a lifetime, and who do not find going in and out of marriages appealing.

There are many persons who are not "nesters," who do not wish to live under the same roof with a mate.

This is not necessarily a pattern of withdrawal. One former patient of mine is always involved in causes, in addition to his work, and chooses not to marry or to see an intimate every day. The quality of his intimate relationships is excellent, and he puts himself totally into a relationship when the intimate is there. His intimate does not feel deserted when he gives himself to causes and work, since physical separateness is maintained most of the time.

Doris, an acquaintance, resists pressure to marry, or even to have a steady intimate, since she is happy with several male friends. As an airline stewardess, she is able to have significant friends and intimates in several locations from the East to the West Coast. She will change when it is *her* decision, rather than respond to pressure from social expectations.

The key is: Is your decision to marry really your own, carefully considered?

Here, Path Two emerges: the selection of the right intimate for you. Engage your mind as well as your emotions before a commitment to an intimate takes place, and you will have more intimacy success.

PATH TWO

Selecting a Compatible Intimate

Even the most polished human relations skills are not enough to assure successful intimacy with incompatible personalities, or with compatible personalities that are not growth-oriented.

Therefore, a growth orientation *is* the single most important intimacy selection factor.

A commitment to one's growth, and the growth of one's mate, should be part of any commitment to intimacy. Other variables, such as similarity of education, interests, social patterns, and sexual compatibility, are also important. But the quality of caring that takes place in a relationship where self- and other-person growth is a goal creates a situation where individual differences and similarities work together to enrich everyone.

Since we are also individuals separate from our parents, Path Three will help us write our own life-lines.

PATH THREE

Your Own Intimacy Script

As we mature, new appreciation for what we have learned from our parents becomes more evident. It is a supreme compliment to parents when we choose our own vocation, our friends, and the lifestyle that best suits our intimacy. Like each individual, each intimacy is unique and should follow a path separate from one's parents, in spite of the fact that parents serve as our most powerful models of the way to live.

I have listened to countless persons in psychotherapy reevaluate their approach to an intimate in order to determine whether they are following a parental script or writing their own life-lines. The real issue is whether the choice is their own. Many times a person wants to establish caring similar to what his parents experienced, but the choice must be a conscious one rather than an automatic pattern.

When a choice is conscious, an intimate carries it out with more enthusiasm and conviction. Talk openly to your intimate about habits and patterns you take for granted to see if you really want to keep old patterns. Do not be afraid to try new habits to see if they fit you and your intimate. It might take several months, or even years, to rethink how you want to live, but the time is worth it to your intimacy. Your actual experience is the best teacher, and false starts can be easily corrected with open, honest communication and the acceptance stressed in Path Four.

Path Four

Intimate Acceptance Releases Growth Forces

By research we have established that acceptance, more than any single variable, releases growth forces in the person accepted. Attempts to "remake" an intimate are destructive. The world-renowned psychologist Carl Rogers concludes, after forty years of psychotherapy research and practice, that our communication is never neutral in terms of impact on another person's growth. We either block growth or help growth, depending on the quality of acceptance that reaches the other person.

Simple? Not really. As any psychotherapist in training finds out, we are trained in many ways to be intolerant, and most of us in growing up have had little or no training in how to accept other people in a way that releases growth forces. We can disagree with people, even not like most things about them, without rejecting them.

And what we do not like about an intimate can be communicated openly without destructive effects only in a context of real personal acceptance. So I recommend Path Four as a foundation for a dynamic intimacy that will generate excitement.

Also, do not forget to apply this principle to yourself. So often we treat an intimate the way we treat ourselves on the inside. Each day reaffirm your self-acceptance until you feel it inside. Then you will be better able to accept your intimate in a more profound way. Accept yourself *and* your intimate.

Acceptance leads naturally to the person-centered expression of sex of Path Five.

PATH FIVE

Person-Centered Sex

When our intimate treats us as a person with feelings, communication is open and sexual aliveness will tend to be sustained over the years. Technique has its place, but it is not *central* to sexual enjoyment. Otherwise, a complex computer, programmed with all the latest sexual know-how and techniques, would be a better lover than you or I.

Positive sexual attitudes, which have been spelled out in this book, show up in behavior that adds joy to sex. There can be a higher degree of meaning and enjoyment in sex with an intimate than in casual relationships, but there is also more likelihood of exposure to problems in intimacy, and problems affect sexual pleasure. When a sexual relationship with an intimate starts to go downhill, first investigate the relationship for problems—not the need to vary sexual positions in intercourse. When sex is depersonalized by the treatment of persons as things, sex can never be good for long.

Extremes depersonalize sex. Puritanized sex negates sexual enjoyment and splits off sex from normal communication, while an "anything goes" attitude in sex tends to sanction bizarre and abnormal patterns which dehumanize people. The person-centered sex of Path Five allows for individual differences and a wide range of choices, and it is not only sane but practical. That is, sexual joy contributes to a successful intimacy, which in turn helps sustain sexual joy.

When intimacy joy is lost permanently in a relationship, Path Six allows intimates the opportunity to find successful intimacy elsewhere.

Path Six

Divorce for Intimacy Success

After months, years, or decades in an intimacy, some persons must part ways if mutual deprivation is to be avoided and a new success in intimacy is to be experienced. This is sad to talk about, especially for those with a long-term intimacy and possibly children, but sometimes it is the best solution. Isn't the mourning period at the end of an intimacy still briefer and less painful than the prolonged human misery of two persons staying together when the intimacy is dead?

Knowing how to "turn loose" an intimate in small ways, or in a big way when divorce occurs, is essential to intimacy and takes us to Path Seven, which points the way toward a non-possessive intimacy.

Path Seven

Intimacy Open and Experienced

Paradoxically, it is only when we exist as separate individuals that we can risk deep union in intimacy. When we love without possessing, we exorcize fears in intimacy, with personal growth and an alive intimacy the end result.

When we violate the integrity of an intimate by treating him or her as a possession, we trap ourselves in a relationship that has no place to go. Instead of preserving the relationship, a "you belong to me" attitude eliminates joy and stifles growth.

Separate friends and separate interests are part of a healthy relationship and will enrich the lives of both intimates. Possessiveness in intimacy creates an insecurity where almost anything that happens endangers the relationship.

Intimacy, open and experienced, is our ideal, but this is more a direction than a destination. Each intimacy has a unique style of its own, and the intimates need to decide how much openness and separateness is right for them at any given time.

In other words, "openness" as a technique won't work unless you are *ready* to allow your intimacy to open up more to outside influences. Honest communication with your intimate will help you decide how much separateness is good for your relationship. This path allows for continuing change, and openness to change is the real basis for security. It is also essential to Path Eight: a growing intimacy.

PATH EIGHT

Intimacy Alive and Changing

Studies show, and trained psychotherapists know, that intimacy will naturally flow through stages of change. Studies also show that a static intimacy will never "grow up" to become more than two persons clinging to each other for security reasons. Therefore, we block or inhibit change in intimacy at our own peril.

If change somehow means that you and your intimate should separate—a common fear—you can better tolerate this than a static state of existing together. But change need not mean separation. We can be prepared for the stages of change in intimacy and learn to encourage change. We can also expect change in our intimate over time, and this is the concern of Path Nine.

Path Nine

Intimacy Joy
and
Personal Growth

Behavioral science teaches us that personality is never static, and that problems occur as a result of personality maturation being blocked. Intimacy is one special situation that can help destroy blocks to personality growth from the past as well as the present. If we *expect* our intimate to change, and assist that change, our reward will be a better intimacy.

As intimates, we have a powerful influence on each other. Resisting growth in an intimate is harmful to him or her. As we accept personality change as a fact of life, we will assist, not fight, change in our intimate. We can then share the excitement of new expressions and new interests that persons who change bring to a relationship.

Path Ten's unconditional love is a primary way to release growth forces in an intimate.

Path Ten

Love Without Strings

We can learn to give love without trying to manipulate the response of an intimate. Patterns of control which block the natural flow of love are thus broken. Instead of wondering "Has he or she given enough to me?" we can give love to the point that love exists in its own right. At that point we *become* love, and when we have done this (as idealistic as it may sound), we will not want to deny that part of our existence.

Real strength in a relationship is manifest when intimates give love without strings attached and would leave the intimacy before they would allow controls to develop. Countless hours of psychotherapy often take place before a person realizes that deceptions, games, and manipulations block the very intimacy that all of us need.

Once we accept the idea that such games have no winners, movement toward unconditional love is assured. And each partner is strengthened and will grow, independently of the response of the intimate.

Responsibility for one's intimate has definite limits, especially when happiness is the issue. This is the focus of Path Eleven.

PATH ELEVEN

Happiness as Self-Discovery

You can contribute to the happiness of your intimate, but you probably cannot make an intimate happy. Happiness for each of us is an inner state discovered by our own efforts.

Our intimate has the right to choose to live in a manner that results in unhappiness. That is his or her responsibility. Your responsibility is to choose the right paths for your own happiness. This is not a self-centered position, but one that maximizes your impact for good on those around you.

Outside events cannot create happiness for you. Happiness is a by-product of right choices in your life and a way of judging whether you are headed in the right direction. So follow the way that generates most consistently a state of inner joy, and you will be doing the best for yourself and your intimate.

I am convinced, after fifteen years of psychotherapy practice, that we should expect to enjoy intimacy most of the time for most of our lives. And this is the message of Path Twelve.

Path Twelve

Expect Intimacy Success

We must be convinced that we can have success in intimacy most of the time, and we need not settle for less. The expectation of success, Path Twelve, is a reasonable one when we are able to spot obstacles to intimacy and remove or surmount them. But false ideas about human relationships are still widespread and needlessly leave a wake of crushed hopes and disillusionment.

Nature has already built into us what it takes to enjoy intimacy, and the psychological sciences have given us the tools to use these inborn resources. This book is written with the conviction that persons without professional training can use what has been learned about intimate relationships for success in intimacy now! The time *is* now for every person to enjoy intimacy more!

The possibility of a future where we can experience intimacy success far beyond our present dreams is on the horizon, and this book is a map for your journey to success.

12 | Total-Person Growth Enriches Intimacy

I would also like to recommend meditation to aid your total personal growth and to enrich your present intimacy. First, however, I would like to share with you an assumption that I make about the nature of individuals.

Men and women are more to me than personalities with complex, computer-like brains that exist for a flicker in the vast expanse of time. There is to me the unique person that exists beyond space and time, and which continues to exist, building on the lessons of this life. This belief gives added meaning to personal growth, since the value of growth is not lost at the grave. Therefore, total-person growth must include the spiritual dimension of existence. Self-actualized persons, in Maslow's study, invariably have had a spiritual experience, a turning point in their self-development.

Perhaps meditation, which is centuries old and is used in almost every culture, will be the way for us to tap a level of altered consciousness where spiritual experience is possible. And the techniques of meditation combined with new facts from brain research on altered consciousness, especially with the alpha level of awareness, may provide a potent tool for human growth.

Also, we should not place an arbitrary limit on potential growth. Recent research on the human brain indicates that the right side of our brain has been virtually ignored, yet it is the seat of intuitive powers and a type of knowledge that may transcend any of the language or cognitive learning that is localized on the left side of the brain. Psychologist Robert Ornstein of the Institute for the Study of Human Consciousness, at Langley Porter Neuropsychiatric Institute, points out that meditation changes the usual waking level of awareness so that another level of consciousness emerges. This level, called intuition, is a function of the right hemisphere of the brain.

After a year's study of meditation, psychologist Charles Tart observed that greater sensitivities, a calmer mind, and more energy resulted from meditation. Other studies in university settings indicate that consistent meditators, compared to a control group of non-meditators, are happier, more relaxed, more inner-directed, and have developed deeper personal relationships.

My own personal experience with meditation this year parallels the results of studies mentioned. Meditation has helped me, as well as some of my patients, to experience increased emotional awareness, beyond the intellectual processes. Results so far suggest that meditation might be a valuable tool for intimates to use on their own.

There are many different meditation techniques, but generally there is concentration on a specific focus, such as a visual image, a sound, or abdominal breathing while in a motionless position, until the mind is quiet. If the brain waves slow to alpha (about 8–13 cycles per second), perception seems to be expanded; and visual imagery, or just an absence of throught processes, may occur. Specific problems can be meditated upon, and sometimes answers emerge in symbolic form or by visual imagery. Meditation at the very least can help persons cope with the stresses of modern life and can create a more relaxed atmosphere for intimates.

We all need the satisfaction of intimate relationships for personality growth, as well as for survival. Study, prayer, meditation, open communication, and psychotherapy can help us travel along the twelve paths to intimacy.

Intimates are the building blocks of society; when intimacy failure is widespread, society degenerates. I believe that the way is clear to establish a new order of enlightened intimacy which can create currents of love throughout a society that needs it now. A loving relationship transforms the persons involved; and if enough persons become buoyed by intimacy success, the energy generated could help eradicate inhumanity to man and create a world where human growth is the norm.

Bibliography

Ackerman, Nathan W. *The Psychodynamics of Family Life: Diagnosis and Treatment of Family Life.* New York: Basic Books, Inc., 1958.

Adler, Alfred. *The Practice and Theory of Individual Psychology.* New York: Harcourt, 1927.

Allport, Gordon. *Becoming: Basic Considerations for a Psychology of Personality.* New Haven: Yale University Press, 1955.

————. *Personality and Social Encounter.* Boston: Beacon Press, 1964.

————. *The Nature of Personality: Selected Papers.* Cambridge, Mass.: Addison and Wesley, 1950.

Bach, George R., and Peter Wyden. *The Intimate Enemy.* New York: William Morrow and Co., Inc., 1969.

Baruch, Dorothy Walter, and Hyman Miller. *Sex in Marriage: New Understandings.* Harper and Brothers, 1962.

Berne, Eric. *Games People Play.* New York: Grove Press, 1964.

Cuber, John F. with Peggy B. Harroff. *Sex and the Significant Americans.* Baltimore: Penguin Books, 1966.

Erikson, Erik H. *Identity and the Life Cycle.* New York: International Universities Press, 1967.

Ferguson, Marilyn. *The Brain Revolution.* New York, N.Y.: Taplinger Publishing Co., 1973.

Ginott, Haim G. *Between Parent and Child.* New York: The Macmillan Company, 1965.

Greene, Bernard L. *The Psychotherapies of Marital Disharmony.* New York: The Free Press, 1965.

Jourard, Sidney M. *The Transparent Self,* Princeton, N.J.: D. Van Nostrand Company, Inc., 1968.

Kinsey, Alfred C., Wardell B. Pomeroy, and Clyde E. Martin. *Sexual Behavior in the Human Male.* Philadelphia: W. B. Saunders Company, 1948.

————, and Paul H. Gebhard. *Sexual Behavior in the Human Female.* Philadelphia: W. B. Saunders Company, 1953.

Lederer, William J., and Don D. Jackson. *The Mirages of Marriage.* New York: W. W. Norton & Company, Inc., 1968.

MacGregor, Robert. *Multiple Impact Therapy with Families.* New York: McGraw-Hill, 1964.

Maslow, Abraham. *Motivation and Personality.* New York: Harper & Row, 1954.

————. *Toward a Psychology of Being.* 2d ed. Princeton, N.J.: D. Van Nostrand Company, Inc., 1968.

Masters, William, and Virginia E. Johnson. *Human Sexual Response.* Boston: Little, Brown and Company, 1966.

————. *Human Sexual Inadequacy.* Boston: Little, Brown and Company, 1970.

May, Rollo. *Love and Will.* New York: W. W. Norton & Company, Inc., 1969.

McCary, James Leslie. *Human Sexuality: Physiological and Psychological Factors of Sexual Behavior.* Princeton, N.J.: D. Van Nostrand Company, Inc., 1967.

Mead, Margaret. *Sex and Temperament in Three Primitive Societies.* New York: Dell Publishing Company, Inc., 1968.

Miller, Keith. *The Taste of New Wine.* Waco, Texas: Word Books, Inc., 1965.

Montagu, Ashley. *The Natural Superiority of Women.* Rev. ed. New York: Collier Books, 1970.

Murphy, Gardner, and F. Jensen. *Approaches to Personality.* New York: Coward, 1932.

O'Neill, George and Nena. *Open Marriage: A New Life Style for Couples.* New York: M. Evans & Co., 1972.

Ornstein, Robert E. *The Psychology of Consciousness.* New York, N.Y.: The Viking Press, 1972.

Parsons, Talcott, and Robert F. Bales. *Family Socialization and Interaction Process.* Glencoe, Ill.: The Free Press, 1955.

Perls, Frederick S. *Gestalt Therapy Verbatim.* Lafayette, Cal.: Real People Press, 1969.

Pines, Maya. *The Brain Changers.* New York, N.Y.: Harcourt Brace Jovanovich, Inc., 1973.

Reuben, David. *Everything You Always Wanted to Know About Sex but Were Afraid to Ask.* New York: David McKay Company, 1969.

Rogers, Carl R. *On Becoming a Person.* Boston: Houghton Mifflin Company, 1961.

————. *On Encounter Groups.* New York: Harper & Row, 1970.

Shostrom, Everett, and James Kavanaugh. *Between Man and Woman.* Los Angeles: Nash Publishing, 1971.

Slater, Philip E. *The Pursuit of Loneliness: American Culture at the Breaking Point.* Boston: Beacon Press, 1970.

Toffler, Alvin. *Future Shock.* New York: Bantam Books, Inc., 1971.

Viorst, Judith. *Yes, Married: A Saga of Love and Complaint.* New York: Saturday Review Press, 1972.

Winter, Gibson. *Love and Conflict: New Patterns in Family Life.* New York: Doubleday, 1958.